Ma...

MW00776853

MARY'S MIRACLES

A Traveler's Guide to

CATHOLIC AMERICA

MARION AMBERG

Our Sunday Visitor
Huntington, Indiana

Except where noted, the Scripture citations used in this work are taken from the *Revised Standard Version of the Bible — Second Catholic Edition*, copyright © 1965, 1966, 2006 National Council of the Churches of Christ in the United States of America. Used by permission. All rights reserved.

Every reasonable effort has been made to determine copyright holders of excerpted materials and to secure permissions as needed. If any copyrighted materials have been inadvertently used in this work without proper credit being given in one form or another, please notify Our Sunday Visitor in writing so that future printings of this work may be corrected accordingly.

Copyright © 2022 by Marion Amberg

27 26 25 24 23 22   1 2 3 4 5 6 7 8 9

All rights reserved. With the exception of short excerpts for critical reviews, no part of this work may be reproduced or transmitted in any form or by any means whatsoever without permission from the publisher. For more information, visit: www.osv.com/permissions.

Our Sunday Visitor Publishing Division
Our Sunday Visitor, Inc.
200 Noll Plaza
Huntington, IN 46750
www.osv.com
1-800-348-2440

ISBN: 978-1-68192-933-0 (Inventory No. T2674)
1. TRAVEL—Special Interest—Religious.
2. TRAVEL—United States—General.
3. RELIGION—Christianity—Catholic.

eISBN: 978-1-68192-934-7
LCCN: 2022937857

Cover and interior design: Amanda Falk
Cover art: AdobeStock; courtesy Our Lady of Peace Church and Shrine, Santa Clara, California: "The Awesome Madonna"

PRINTED IN THE UNITED STATES OF AMERICA

To Maria Hilf,
who delivered the town of
Amberg, Germany,
from the Black Death in 1634.
Without her miraculous intervention,
I might not be here today.

CONTENTS

INTRODUCTION

America loves Mary — and Mary loves America!

You'll find Mary's love all across our great land: in wee chapels and grand basilicas, in hillside grottos and on a tiny island, even in a ghost town. Erected in fulfillment of a vow, Our Lady of the Rockies at Butte, Montana, is the third tallest statue in the country! What do all these legendary sites have in common? Miracles wrought by Mary's intercession.

According to the glossary of the *Catechism of the Catholic Church*, a miracle is "a sign or wonder, such as a healing or the control of nature, which can only be attributed to divine power." Catholics don't pray to Mary, but we do ask her intercession. Just like we might ask a friend or a relative to storm heaven for us in times of need, we ask Mary to intercede on our behalf. You have no greater friend or a more powerful prayer ally than the Blessed Mother. She takes your problems straight to Jesus, like she did at the Cana wedding feast when Jesus turned the water into wine (Jn 2:1–11). Mary is Jesus' Mama, and it's difficult for kids to say no to Mama! And who knows Jesus better than his Mama? She carried him in her womb and taught him the Jewish ABCs.

In Cold Spring, Minnesota, "Miracle Mary" averted a locust plague and then eradicated the species. When the ragtag American army defeated the well-fortified British navy at the Battle of New Orleans in 1815 — a battle that lasted all of thirty minutes — the victory was ascribed to Our Lady of Prompt Succor. At Key West, Florida, Mary Star of the Sea stops hurricanes.

Ave Maria!

Mother Mary intercedes for the sick, stops fires in their tracks, drills for gas, and is one tough real estate agent. At Carey, Ohio, Mary the Wonderworker helped catch a thief who confessed to robbing over 7,000 churches! During World War II, the congregations of four unrelated parishes gathered weekly to pray the "War Rosary" for their soldiers in harm's way. Every soldier at these four parishes came home alive!

Irish, German, Spanish, French, Sicilian, Native American, Black, Lebanese, Belgian, Ukrainian, Acadian, Cuban, Polish, Asian, Italian, Mexican — Our Lady loves us all.

The fifty-two stories in this book are but a fraction of Mary's miracles in Catholic America. Some will make you laugh or cry. Yet others will leave your jaw hanging wide open. One drinking man quit the bottle when he saw Our Lady's chapel floating in the air! And after a Colorado church fire, a multi-pointed crown of soot was found on a painting of the Blessed Mother — over her head, just like it belonged there. Some Marian stories are lost to history, others are hidden and known only to the people themselves. Still other stories are yet to be written by you — if you call on Mary.

You don't need to travel to Europe or around the world to visit a great Marian shrine. Graces abound at the National Shrine of Our Lady of Good Help in Champion, Wisconsin, the only Church-approved Marian apparition site in America. You'll also find incredible miracles and stories of Mary's love from Massachusetts to California, Georgia to Alaska, and everywhere in between. Where Mary is revered, miracles follow.

Be inspired.

Come to Mary.

HOW TO USE
THIS BOOK

You can use this book in several ways: as a road guide to Our Lady's miracle sites across Catholic America, as an armchair traveler in a "stay-pilgrimage," or as a spiritual sojourner wanting to learn more about Our Lady's fabulous intercession. Because the book features fifty-two miracle sites, you can also use it as a devotional. Each week, pick a site and learn more about Mary and her titles. The devotions could be done individually, as a family, or in a group.

No matter how you use the book, come to Mary and ask her to intercede for your own needs. Your miracle may be only a prayer away.

This book is divided into seven geographic regions, with maps giving the locations of miracle sites for that region. Each site is assigned a number; the index uses these site numbers instead of page numbers for easier reference.

The stories for each geographic section are arranged by state and presented in a feature story format. Many of the longer stories include two sidebars. The first sidebar, Signs and Wonders, gives fascinating trivia or testimonies of Mary's miraculous intervention. A second sidebar provides a brief history of Mary's appellation for that site, e.g., Our Lady of Providence at Saint Mary-of-the-Woods, Indiana. Also presented throughout the book are shorter stories of lesser-known sites — but "lesser known" doesn't mean "less than." Your head will spin at the wonders of Mary's love across America!

Websites, telephone numbers, physical addresses, and other pertinent information are given to help you find your way to Mary. If you're looking for a book or resource on a particular site, consult the Resources secton starting on page 335.

Luring you to Our Lady are photos of her miracle chapels and shrines. Some photos are images of the Madonna under her patronal titles, others are photos of the sites themselves. Some images are historical, others are contemporary. Mary is timeless and so are her miracles.

If you're looking for a Marian site under a specific title, check the index. Here you'll find all of the Marian appellations featured in the book and their corresponding holy sites.

Let's go visit Mary!

NORTHEAST

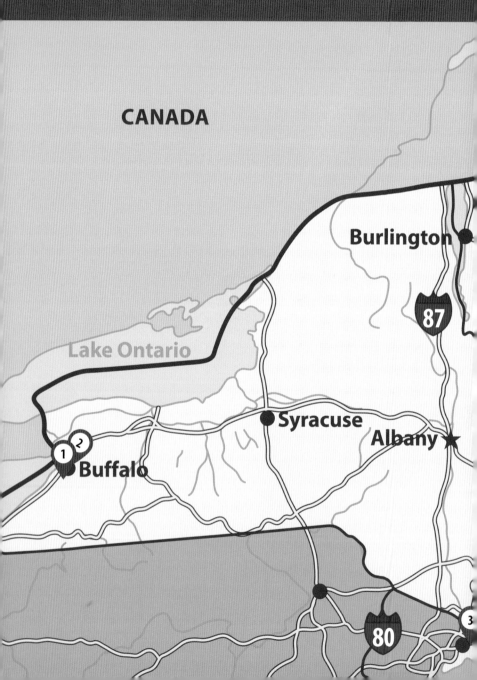

CANADA

Burlington

87

Lake Ontario

Syracuse

Albany ★

Buffalo

80

3

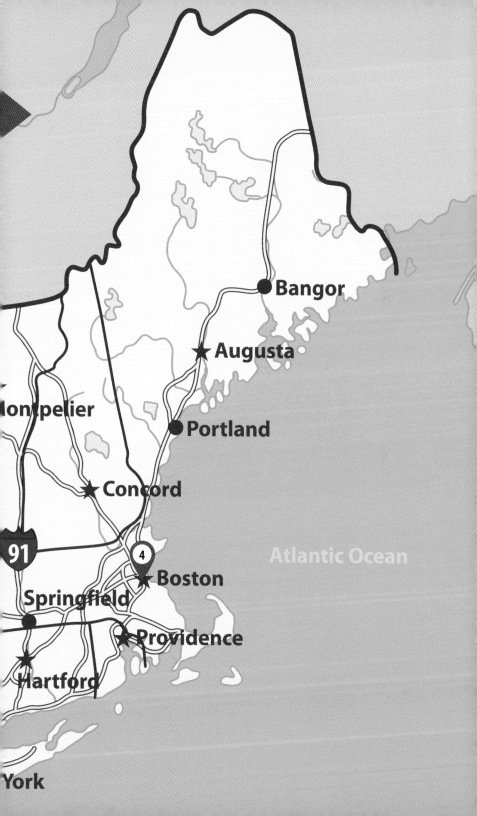

New York

① LACKAWANNA

In 1921 when Venerable Nelson Baker began building **Our Lady of Victory National Shrine and Basilica** at Lackawanna, near Buffalo in western New York State, he didn't have a nickel. When the magnificent shrine was dedicated on May 25, 1926 (and immediately elevated to a basilica), he didn't owe a penny! The businessman-turned-priest lived on miracles — miracles wrought by Our Lady of Victory. It was a partnership made in heaven.

The second of four sons, Nelson Henry Baker was born on February 16, 1842, to Lewis and Caroline Baker of Buffalo, and baptized as an infant in the Lutheran faith of his German father. When Nelson was nine years old, inspired by his Irish Catholic mother, he was accepted into the Catholic Church. Young Nelson also took a shine to Our Lady. When his parents gave him a dollar to spend as he wished, he didn't buy a new baseball or a bag of marbles, but a statue of the Blessed Mother. It was a portent of things to come.

After high school graduation, Nelson worked in his father's general store and then served a stint in the Union army during the Civil War. Returning to Buffalo, Nelson and a friend launched a successful feed and grain enterprise. The five-foot-four-inch bachelor was no social slouch either: He could sing and play the piano at parties like nobody's business. The young ladies considered him a "real catch."

The ladies never caught Nelson, however. In September 1869, the twenty-seven-year-old convert — nearly ten years older than his classmates — entered Our Lady of the Angels Seminary in Buffalo. Five years later, he took a pilgrimage to the great shrines of Europe. It was at the Basilica of Notre Dame des Victoires (Our Lady of Victories) in Paris, France, that Nelson found "his Lady." Lured by an irresistible statue of Mary holding a little boy, the seminarian knelt before the altar and prayed.

Did Our Lady speak to Nelson at her Parisian altar? That's not recorded in history, but something mystical surely happened. Nelson promised Our Lady of Victory to devote his entire life to her service and to spread her devotion in America. When he was beset with problems in the future, Nelson would remember "her silent promise to help him in his work," wrote Floyd Anderson in *Apostle of Charity: The Father Nelson Henry Baker Story*.

Nelson was ordained a priest on March 19, 1876, at age thirty-four. When he arrived at his first assignment as assistant superintendent of Limestone Hill — two institutions for orphaned and wayward boys near Buffalo — he was appalled. St. John's Protectory (for older boys) and St. Joseph's Orphan Asylum (for younger boys) were $27,000 in debt, a pretty penny in the day. Five years later, the debt had ballooned to over $60,000.

Father Baker thought the situation hopeless and was granted a transfer. A year later, the priest with a "head for numbers" was sent back to Limestone Hill as superintendent and to St. Patrick's Church as pastor. He was here to stay.

Creditors lined up at Father Baker's door. The savvy priest asked if they would take partial payment and wait for the rest. If they did, he would do business with them again. If not, he would pay them and their business relationship was over. Father Baker then climbed into his horse and buggy, drove to his bank, and withdrew his personal savings to pay off whatever debt he could.

There were still outstanding bills. What to do? Father Baker turned to Our Lady of Victory, and the miracles began. He wrote hundreds of letters to postmasters around the country asking for names of charitable Catholic ladies. When the postmasters responded with names, he wrote thousands more letters to these ladies and asked them to support the boys in his care. Would they join the Association of Our Lady of Victory? And tell their friends? Annual membership dues: twenty-five cents. Father Baker's "direct marketing" campaign, and later his publications, were a huge success!

Father Baker not only paid off the debt, but also expanded Limestone Hill. He built a trade school for boys, Our Lady of Victory Infant Home for unwed mothers and their babies, and Our Lady of Victory Hospital. As his fame grew, so did the number of orphans arriving at "the Hill." Some came by train, with just a tag hanging from a coat button: "Father Baker in New York."

One night when Father Baker was paying the Hill's sky-high heating and lighting bills, he had a flash of inspiration. What if he drilled for natural gas on the Hill to supply the needed heat and light? Natural gas had been found across the border in Canada and in limited amounts around Buffalo. Father Baker went to Our Lady of Victory in prayer — and then to the bishop. Was it a coincidence the bishop had just received $5,000 from a donor for a special diocesan project? Father Baker didn't think so. He left with $2,000 in his pocket.

When the drillers arrived in January 1891, they gawked as a procession of altar boys, religious sisters and brothers, and Father Baker walked the grounds with lighted candles, singing and praying the Rosary. Then Father Baker stopped, sprinkled the ground with holy water, and buried a small statue of Our Lady.

"Drill here," he instructed, "but try not to disturb the statue."

The drillers drilled and drilled, then drilled some more. But no gas was found. Out of money, Father Baker went back to the bishop and extracted the remaining $3,000 of the donor's special gift. Scoffers began calling the dig "Father Baker's Folly." Finally, on August 21, at a depth of 1,137 feet, the drillers hit gas! Victoria Well is still producing today.

Decades passed, and Father Baker still dreamed of a fitting tribute for his Lady. In 1921, the energetic seventy-nine-year-old began his monument: A shrine that would rival the great churches of Europe. Constructed of forty-six different marbles and neo-Renaissance in design, Our Lady of Victory National Shrine and Basilica is indeed magnificent.

Standing on the 165-foot-tall copper dome (the second largest US dome at the time), four eighteen-foot copper angels sound the trumpet to the north, south, east, and west.

Step inside, and you're off to paradise. Some two thousand angels in every possible line of sight decorate the interior — angel water fonts, angel musicians, adoring angels, even "angels of the stairs" holding light fixtures to illuminate the steps. Adorning the eighty-foot-diameter dome mural, depicting the Assumption and Coronation of the Blessed Mother, is another heavenly host. The babies and little ones at the Infant Home served as angelic models.

While Father Baker oversaw every shrine detail — from the nine-foot marble statue of Our Lady of Victory on the main altar, to the life-size marble Stations of the Cross, to the superb stained-glass windows — there's one "small detail" that didn't go according to plan. To honor the religious men and women at Limestone Hill, Father Baker commissioned two white marble sculptures to top the colonnades of the main entrance. One sculpture would feature a flock of children with a nun to represent the Sisters of St. Joseph; the other sculpture, with more children and a male religious, would honor priests and the Brothers of the Holy Infancy. Both sculptures included a gargantuan guardian angel protecting their charges.

When the Italian sculptures arrived in Lackawanna, Father Baker was livid. Instead of a male religious, his own likeness had been carved in stone! As the story goes, the sisters and the brothers (perhaps

Exterior of Our Lady of Victory National Shrine
and Basilica — Lackawanna, New York

even Our Lady herself) conspired to memorialize the humble priest, who preferred the unassuming title of Father over Monsignor.

"While Father Baker inspected the artists' work day after day, a young Italian sculptor would be hiding in the shadows, modeling his face in clay," continued Anderson. The model was sent to Italy, where carvers chiseled the priest's image in stone.

Our Lady of Victory Shrine was consecrated on May 25, 1926, and designated America's second basilica two months later. Total cost: An estimated $3.2 million. Father Baker began with nary a nickel and finished not owing a penny. Another victory for his Lady!

The Apostle of Charity died July 29, 1936, at age ninety-four. His legacy lives today as OLV Charities and OLV Human Services. In 1999, his remains were re-entombed inside the basilica, at the foot of the Grotto of Our Lady of Lourdes — hewn out of lava rock from Mount Vesuvius in Italy. Father Baker was declared Venerable in 2011.

The Father Baker Museum, in the shrine's lower level, tells his (and Mary's) remarkable story in historical photos, vintage newspaper articles, and artifacts that include his death mask and a cherished statue of Our Lady of Victory.

Come to Mary: 767 Ridge Road, Lackawanna, NY 14218. (716) 828-9444. olvbasilica.org.

Signs and Wonders

Legends abound about Father Baker and his miracle Lady, but none are as mysterious as the story of the four spiraling red marble columns that support the canopy over the main altar of Our Lady of Victory National Shrine and Basilica in Lackawanna. After World War I, one story has it, some soldiers from Buffalo, New York, were traveling in Spain and happened upon a farmer's cottage. When the Americans stepped inside, they were astounded to find images of Our Lady of Victory and Father Baker.

When the soldiers told the old farmer they knew Father Baker and that he wanted to build a beautiful shrine of many marbles to Our Lady, the farmer became quite elated. He had rare red marble on his land that nobody wanted to quarry. Father Baker could have the marble for free!

How did the old Spanish farmer know Father Baker? How did it happen that he had red marble nobody wanted? And just enough red marble for the four columns? As Father Baker once said of Our Lady, "She does it all."

• • • • •

When people with health ailments or fiscal woes came to Father Baker for prayer, the bespectacled priest would look them in the eye, pat them on the cheek, and say, "Don't worry. Our Lady will take care of you." And Our Lady did.

One day the inexplicable happened. Nurse Clark, who worked at Our Lady of Victory Infant Home, fell gravely ill. She was growing worse by the day. One night a doctor pronounced Nurse Clark dead and covered her face with a cloth. The other nurses began to weep, when in walked Father Baker. He took the cloth off Nurse Clark's face, took her hand, and keeping his fingers on her pulse, began to pray the Rosary.

When the Rosary was finished, Father Baker told a nurse to take the dead woman's pulse. The skeptical nurse did as she was told and nearly dropped over dead herself. Nurse Clark was alive!

• • • • •

Even after his death, Father Baker would appear out of nowhere to pray with people. The story is told of two women praying in the basilica when the saintly priest happened by. One woman, deaf in one ear, told him about her affliction. He laid his hands on her head and appealed to Our Lady of Victory. When the woman left the church, she could hear an angel feather drop.

Our Lady of Victory

If you need a dramatic rescue, turn to Our Lady of Victory! On October 7, 1571, she helped a small Christian fleet defeat a much larger Muslim force in the naval Battle of Lepanto — a victory credited to the power of praying the Rosary. King Louis XIII of France also invoked Our Lady in battle. In 1629, in gratitude for his triumph over the Huguenots at La Rochelle, the king laid the first stone for today's Basilica of Notre Dame des

Victoires in Paris.

Many future saints came to that historic shrine to pray. It's said that John Henry Newman gave thanks here for his conversion to the Catholic Faith, and young Thérèse of Lisieux prayed before Our Lady's statue for help in her vocation as a Carmelite nun. Venerable Nelson Baker visited the shrine twice on his European pilgrimage in 1874.

The feast of Our Lady of Victory, commonly known as Our Lady of the Rosary, is celebrated on October 7 — the date of her miraculous win at Lepanto.

CHEEKTOWAGA

Can Our Lady take the world by storm? You'll say yes after visiting the **Historic Shrine of Maria Hilf** (German for "Mary's Help") in Cheektowaga, near Buffalo in western New York State.

On November 11, 1836, Joseph Batt, his wife Barbara, and eight of their nine children, all of Alsace-Lorraine, boarded the ship *Mary Ann* for America. (Their oldest child, Joseph, was already in New York.) Nineteen days later, the ship encountered a storm of hurricane magnitude. The *Mary Ann* was stripped of its sails and masts, and began taking on water. Would the ship and her passengers sink to a watery grave?

Batt, a God-fearing man, turned his sights to heaven. Invoking Our Lady under the titles of Mary, Star of the Sea (see Key West, Florida, site 14) and Mary, Help of Christians, he vowed to build her a chapel in exchange for his family's safe passage to the New World. How could Our Lady refuse? The ship's very name *Mary Ann* entreated two powerful intercessors: the Virgin Mary and her mother, Saint Ann, patroness of sailors and protector against storms.

"And behold his prayers were heard," noted *The Chapel*, "for though experienced seamen had given up all hope the storm subsided." The crew rigged an improvised sail and the ship drifted to Ireland, where it was repaired. The *Mary Ann* sailed again and docked in New York on February 2 — Candlemas Day, feast of the Purification of the Blessed Virgin Mary.

The Batt family bought land at Cheektowaga

Mary, Star of the Sea, painting commissioned by Joseph Batt
— Historic Shrine of Maria Hilf, Cheektowaga, New York

and settled down as farmers. The years slid by, but Batt, a stone mason in the Old World, did not forget his oceanic promise. In 1851, Batt, now sixty-two years old, deeded land to the Diocese of Buffalo for a chapel and began making his own bricks. The Historic Shrine of Maria Hilf, as it's now called, was dedicated on October 2, 1853, the feast of Our Lady of the Rosary (then celebrated on the first Sunday in October, and later moved to October 7).

The small chapel soon became a pilgrimage destination. A cholera epidemic in 1854 sent settlers of Alsatian, Bavarian, Swiss, and Rhinelander heritage to the feet of Mary, soliciting her protection from the deadly scourge. In 1864, Fr. Joseph Zoegel, pastor in nearby Williamsville, promoted pilgrimages here to pray for the end of America's Civil War. The pilgrimage on V-J Day (August 15, 1945) was unlike any before: It was jubilant! Throngs of grateful pilgrims stretched from the chapel into downtown Buffalo, a distance of nine miles. World War II was over!

The chapel even drew future saints. St. John Neumann, Bishop of the Diocese of Philadelphia, dedicated the chapel in 1853. Saint Frances Xavier Cabrini (see Golden, Colorado, site 42) came here in the early twentieth century, and Ven. Nelson Baker, known for his devotion to Our Lady of Victory (see Lackawanna, New York, site 1), advocated for the chapel's preservation when others wanted to tear the miracle shrine down.

The chapel was enlarged in 1871, and again in 1926. Batt's original chapel is now the sanctuary. Above the altar hangs a large, ominous oil painting, commissioned by Batt. Mary, Star of the Sea is seated in a cloud; the Child Jesus, securely anchored in her arms, stands on her left knee. Both are peering down at a storm-tossed ship. The painting begs the question: What if Joseph Batt hadn't invoked Mary's help? Would the chapel of miracles be here today? But he did, and the rest is her-story.

The chapel grounds includes numerous grottoes and a cemetery where Batt, his family, and many early settlers rest.

Come to Mary: 4125 Union Road, Cheektowaga, NY 14225. (716) 276-9288. ourladyhelpofchristians .org.

Signs and Wonders

The Historic Shrine of Maria Hilf in Cheektowaga is a miracle house. So many cures and favors happened here that a Buffalo newspaper in 1894 called the chapel "a second Lourdes." The cures, especially the healings of children, are out of this world.

Shortly after the shrine opened in 1853, reported *The Chapel*, a child was cured of "severe ulcers and deformity." In 1859, a ten-year-old boy was healed of articular disease. Seven years later, a nine-year-old girl's eye affliction vanished after praying in the chapel.

Chapel founder Joseph Batt's own grandson was healed in 1865 of a mangled arm, the result of an accident. When a wheel of a heavy wagon crushed the boy's arm, the doctor wanted to amputate the limb. The Batt family wouldn't hear of it. They had recourse to Our Lady Help of Christians and ran straight to the chapel to pray. Shortly thereafter, the boy's arm was good as new.

Our Lady Help of Christians

Mary has been a great help to Christians for millennia, but the feast of Our Lady Help of Christians dates only from 1815 — to satisfy a vow made by Servant of God Pope Pius VII.

The dramatic story begins in 1798, when Napoleon Bonaparte's troops arrested Pope Pius VI. The Pontiff was taken to France, where he died in 1799. On March 21, 1800, Cardinal Barnaba Chiaramonti, OSB, ascended to the papal throne and took the name Pius VII. Because Napoleon's men had seized the gold and jewel-encrusted papal tiaras when they arrested Pius VI, the new pope was crowned with a tiara made of papier-mâché.

In mid-1809, Napoleon's troops kidnapped Pope Pius VII. The Pontiff was held at Savona, near Genoa, Italy, and later in a castle at Fontainebleau, France. The Holy Father promised God to institute a special feast in honor of Mary if he were restored to the Holy See. According to lore, the pope smuggled a message out of the castle cell exhorting Christians everywhere to implore Our Lady Help of Christians for Napoleon's defeat. The emperor abdicated in April 1814, and Pope Pius VII returned to Rome with great fanfare on May 24.

A year later, the Pontiff established the feast of Our Lady Help of Christians on May 24 — the date of his triumphant return to the Holy See.

BROOKLYN

Can Our Lady's miracles cause you to faint? It happened at the **Basilica of Regina Pacis** in Brooklyn. In May 1942, Msgr. Angelo R. Cioffi and all 12,000 Italian parishioners of St. Rosalia Church in Brooklyn made a vow: They pledged to erect a magnificent shrine to Regina Pacis (Latin for "Queen of Peace") for the protection of their men and women at war and for world peace. A $2 million shrine doesn't pay for itself, so the monsignor went about his "appealing" ways, including silent collections. When the offering plates were passed at Mass, he didn't want to hear the clink-clink of coins. Only "silent" paper bills were dropped into the plates.

Dedicated on August 15, 1951, the feast of Mary's Assumption into heaven, the Italian Renaissance shrine is thoroughly Italian and Marian. The façade imitates Italy's Sanctuary of Our Lady of Pompeii and boasts a 150-foot bell tower with three bells christened Ave Maria, Salve Regina, and Regina Pacis. Inside, stained glass "recites" the Litany of Loreto, and a great painting of Regina Pacis hangs over the high altar. According to legend, Monsignor Cioffi didn't like the first painting of Mother and Child, with an olive branch in his hand, so noted artist Ilario Panzironi had to try again. He was ninety-three years old at the time!

Monsignor Cioffi also coaxed the jewelry — wedding rings, lockets, brooches, and bracelets — off the hands and necks of parishioners to make the eighteen-karat gold crowns for the painting of Regina Pacis. On May 24, 1952, Regina Pacis and Child were solemnly crowned. It was the crowning glory of Mary's shrine of peace.

Peace didn't last for long. A week later, the

gem-studded crowns were gone, stolen! People flooded the shrine to pray for the crowns' return. On Sunday, August 18, a special delivery package arrived at the rectory: It was the crowns. Monsignor Cioffi burst into church to announce the fantastic news. "Some applauded, some prayed, some cried, and three fainted," recounted the basilica's website. Newspapers called it the "Miracle of Brooklyn."

The Chapel of Mary, Mother of the Unborn is another basilica legend. Formerly a baptistery, the chapel walls are covered with hundreds of photos of miracle babies and an inscription that reads, "Blessed is the Fruit of Your Womb." One couple prayed here after an ultrasound revealed their unborn baby had no arms and the doctor had advised them to abort. When the baby was born, the ecstatic parents counted two arms and ten fingers!

Come to Mary: 1230 Sixty-Fifth Street, Brooklyn, NY 11219. (718) 236-0909. basilicaofreginapacis .org.

Regina Pacis (Queen of Peace) by Ilario Panzironi — Basilica of Regina Pacis, Brooklyn, New York

BOSTON

4 On August 18, 1883, Grace Hanley, age sixteen, and her family were gathered in today's **Basilica of Our Lady of Perpetual Help** in Boston, praying yet another novena for the girl's healing. For twelve long years they had been praying without ceasing. Would heaven ever answer?

The daughter of Colonel Patrick T. Hanley, a well-known Civil War officer, Grace was four years old when tragedy struck. While play-driving a carriage with her little friends (much like children today pretend to drive a car), Grace fell and struck her lower back on a large rock, cracking a small bone in her spinal column. An abscess later developed around the bone and a wide opening appeared at the top of her head. Doctors tried everything — electricity, ice bags, poultices, even sandbagging Grace in bed — to relieve the intense pain and headaches, but to no avail. Crutches and steel and leather corsets helped the crippled girl sit up and get around.

On August 9, 1883, a Redemptorist priest encouraged Grace to make a novena at the Redemptorist church in Boston dedicated to Our Lady of Perpetual Help. The very next day, Grace, her father, grandmother, aunt, and her sisters and brothers began the novena at the church.

On the ninth and final day of the novena, Grace was in even worse pain as she and her family got into their buggy for church. Grace partook of Communion and was making her Act of Thanksgiving when everything went dark for her. "I thought, perhaps, I was going to faint," testified Grace, her story chronicled in *The Glories of Mary in Boston*, when another sensation "passed through me from head to foot, like a thrill (and something like electricity)." Suddenly, Grace got up and walked to the altar — alone! Her flabbergasted family couldn't believe their eyes.

Grace kept on walking, out the door of the church, into the street, and didn't stop until she reached her "mother's room, up one flight of stairs." Grace was healed, from head to toe.

News of Grace's fantastic cure spread like wildfire, and crowds began following the miracle girl to church. Grace later joined the Sisters of Jesus and Mary and was known as Sr. Mary of Perpetual Help.

Grace wasn't Our Lady's first Boston miracle. The healings began twelve years earlier on Pentecost Sunday, May 28, 1871, when a replica icon of Our Lady of Perpetual Help was solemnly enthroned in a predecessor church. Within days, little Louisa Julia Kohler was healed of a lame foot. Not

a trace of the ailment remained, save for the scars. Folks with every manner of disease and affliction began descending upon Mission Church, as it was called. To accommodate the crowds, a larger Romanesque temple (today's basilica) was erected of puddingstone in 1876. The grand church became a modern-day Pool of Bethsaida. The deaf heard. The blind saw. The lame walked. Cancers vanished.

The blessings of the sick on Wednesday afternoons at 3:00 p.m., the hour of Divine Mercy, were especially efficacious, as were Our Lady's feast days. On December 8, 1891, the feast of the Immaculate Conception, a shriek pierced the church. When Father Corduke went to investigate, the crowd exclaimed, "Seven people cured!" One was a blind girl. The priest opened his breviary, and because the girl couldn't read Latin, told her to spell a word. The first word on the page was "P-a-t-e-r" (Father).

By 1884, the church had documented well over 300 healings. In Our Lady's Shrine, two enormous vases heaped with crutches, braces, and canes give witness to Mary's help. A plaque on one vase reads, "Miss Grace Hanley cured August 18th, 1883."

Newspaper stories of healings drew even more pilgrims to the Boston landmark. In 1901, the *New York Herald* called the church "A Lourdes in the Land of Puritans." One skeptical priest, who doubted the news accounts of vast crowds cramming the church for healing services, went to see for himself, reported *The Glories of Mary in Boston.* "You could

Crutches left as testimony to miraculous healings — Basilica of Our Lady of Perpetual Help, Boston, Massachusetts

walk on the heads of the people," he remarked. "Where are the aisles? All I can see is one impenetrable jam of humanity."

Our Lady of Perpetual Help is indeed a perpetual help! Healings and miracles continue to this day in the Land of the Puritans — a land Mary surely calls her own.

Come to Mary: 1545 Tremont Street, Boston, MA 02120. (617) 445-2600. bostonsbasilica.com.

Signs and Wonders

The cures wrought by Our Lady at Boston's Basilica of Our Lady of Perpetual Help read like a heavenly roll call: They make you stand up and take notice! Dead limbs raised to life. Barren women cuddling newborn babies. Hunchbacks standing straight as a rod. The brokenhearted restored to joy. No petition is too difficult — or too outrageous — for Our Lady and her Son. Prayers go up and favors come down.

In 1896, Mrs. Anna Boyle of Nova Scotia, blinded for nine years because of cataracts, made a novena at the church. After the third visit, recounted *The Glories of Mary in Boston*, she could "thread a needle without the aid of spectacles."

• • • • •

In 1919, a little boy suffering from a case of tongue-tie was set free.

• • • • •

A woman from Norwood, Massachusetts, was suffering from cancer of the nose and face. Doctors cut the growth from her nose, but it returned. She then had the cancer burned with radium. But it grew worse. Another operation was performed.

"This is not noticeable from the outside except for a hole about the size of a dime under my eye," reported the woman in *The Glories of Mary in Boston*, "but on the inside there is a big hole in the roof of my mouth; the bone under my eye is almost gone, and the bone of my nose partly gone."

She was given three weeks to live.

The woman and her family began a novena to Our Lady of Perpetual Help. On a subsequent hospital visit, she heard the phenomenal words: "The cancer is gone!"

Another glory for Mary!

 ## Our Lady of Perpetual Help

The icon of Our Lady of Perpetual Help, painted on wood in Byzantine style at an unknown date, measures about seventeen-by-twenty-one inches. But size doesn't determine miracle power.

According to tradition, a Roman merchant stole the icon about 1498 from a monastery on the Island of Crete, where many miracles were attributed to the image. While sailing to Rome, the merchant and the ship met a terrible storm. Everyone aboard prayed before the image, and the seas calmed. Back in Rome, the merchant hid the icon in his home.

One day, the Blessed Mother appeared in a dream to the man's six-year-old daughter and asked that the icon be placed in Saint Matthew's Church in Rome, located between the basilicas of Saint Mary Major and Saint John Lateran. The icon remained at Saint Matthew's for three centuries. Napoleon's troops destroyed the church in 1798, but the icon was saved.

In the mid-1800s, the Redemptorist Order erected the Church of Saint Alphonsus de Liguori, in honor of their patron saint, on the site of Saint Matthew's Church so highly favored by Mary. In 1866, Pope Pius IX entrusted the icon to the Redemptorists and said, "Wherever you go, make her known to the world."

Copies were made of the icon, blessed, touched to the original, and sent to Redemptorist churches worldwide. One copy arrived at the Church of Our Lady of Perpetual Help in Boston. Miracles began abounding in the Land of the Puritans and haven't stopped.

The icon is more than a pretty face. Our Lady looks intently at viewers, hearing their every word. The Child, sitting in her left arm, peers off to the side. Is he looking into the future — his and ours? Hovering above him, the archangels Michael and Gabriel hold the instruments of his passion. The Child's hands are wrapped around his Mother's right thumb in a double message of sorts.

"Behold the Savior of the world," the Blessed Mother seems to be saying, her thumb inclined toward her Son.

"Behold your Mother," the Savior replies, his thumb also pointing up at her.

The feast of Our Lady of Perpetual Help is June 27.

MID-ATLANTIC

Pittsburgh

Charleston

81

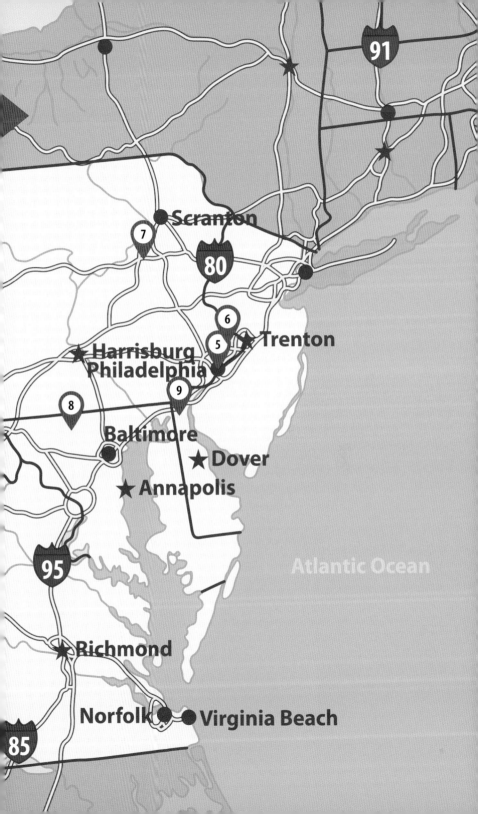

Pennsylvania

(5) PHILADELPHIA

Do Mary's graces ever end? Not at the **Miraculous Medal Shrine** in Philadelphia's Germantown district. The shrine was founded nearly one hundred years ago in 1927, but its roots can be traced back to 1830, when Our Lady appeared to St. Catherine Labouré in Paris, France, and asked her to have the "medal of graces" struck. Miracles and favors have been happening ever since.

The shrine's very own miracle story began in 1890, when Joseph A. Skelly, sixteen years old, was preparing to leave home and enter St. Vincent's Seminary in Germantown. Before Joseph left, his mother hung a Miraculous Medal around his neck and said, "Wear this medal always." Little did she know that one day her son would be placing the medal around hundreds of millions of necks!

Joseph was professed as a Vincentian (also known as the Congregation of the Mission) in 1895 and ordained a priest five years later. Father Skelly served Immaculate Conception Church in Germantown and later as a prefect at St. Vincent's Seminary, where he was known to say, "The chapel is the seminarians' most important classroom." But heaven (and Mary) had a higher calling for the thirty-something priest.

In 1912, Father Skelly was tasked with raising funds to build St. Joseph's College (now closed) in Princeton, New Jersey. As he was preparing the stacks of appeal letters to be mailed, he did a seemingly small thing: He put a Miraculous Medal in each envelope and implored Mary's help. The response was out of this world.

In gratitude, Father Skelly founded the Central Association of the Miraculous Medal (CAMM) in 1915 to promote devotion to Mary and the Miraculous Medal, and became its first director. Twelve years later, in 1927, he built a shrine to Our Lady of the Miraculous Medal in the seminary's Chapel of the Immaculate Conception. The following year, the energetic priest, with dimples that belied his tenacity, launched *The Miraculous Medal* magazine.

Father Skelly didn't stop there. On Monday, December 8, 1930 — feast of the Immaculate Conception and the centenary of Our Lady's apparitions to Catherine Labouré — he initiated the weekly Perpetual Novena to Our Lady of the Miraculous Medal. The novena saw America through the Great Depression and then World War II, when a cavalry of 15,000 prayer warriors descended upon the shrine every Monday to pray for world peace and for soldiers in harm's way. Many soldiers later told inexplicable stories of survival.

The novena advanced around the globe. By 1950,

over 3,300 churches were hosting the novena, with translations in multiple languages, including Braille. Back in Germantown, the Miraculous Medal Shrine became a sort of "dating app": Young men and women began attending the Monday novena with hopes of finding a "good Catholic girl" or a "good Catholic boy." It's said that heaven is filled with marriages made in Germantown!

The Monday novena to Our Lady remains unbroken to this day. During the COVID-19 pandemic, the novena was broadcast via the shrine's website and social media.

Meanwhile, everyone it seems took to wearing the Miraculous Medal. "You see the Medal on countless people at the beaches; on Ringling Brothers, Barnum and Bailey Circus performers, on basketball players in Madison Square Garden, on baseball players at Wrigley Field — and on millions of 'little people' everywhere," reported *The Miraculous Medal*.

When devotees began donating Marian paintings and sculptures to the shrine, Father Skelly opened the Miraculous Medal Art Museum, a collection of over 500 artworks. Ranging in date, technique, origin, and theme, the art presents Mary from a young Virgin, to a nursing Mother, to the Queen of Heaven.

Father Skelly attributed all of the shrine's success to Our Lady, never taking an ounce of credit for himself — but one event is shrine lore. During CAMM's forty-sixth anniversary celebration in 1961, recalled Vincentian Fr. Joseph Dirvin in *The Miraculous Medal*, the eighty-seven-year-old Father Skelly got to his feet and said he wished to live four more years un-

5. Mosaic depicting Our Lady's apparition to St. Catherine Labouré — Miraculous Medal Shrine, Philadelphia, Pennsylvania

til CAMM's fiftieth birthday. The following year, on the forty-seventh anniversary, the aging priest again stood and simply said, "I am just sitting, waiting for the divine call."

At that very instant, the telephone rang!

His "divine call" didn't come that day but on July 8, 1963. During his forty-eight-year tenure as CAMM director, it's estimated the organization distributed seventy-five million Miraculous Medals and forty million booklets and pamphlets. The Miraculous Medal that begot the Miraculous Shrine is still begetting miraculous answers to prayer today. There is no end to Our Lady's stream of graces.

Touring the shrine is like taking a mini-pilgrimage of Chapelle Notre-Dame de la Médaille Miraculeuse in Paris, where Our Lady appeared twice to Daughter of Charity Catherine Labouré. The upper level of the Romanesque-style church holds a replica of the chair that Mary sat in during her first visit, along with a swatch of the original fabric from that chair. The lower level includes an altar that portrays Mary's second visit, also known as the Virgin of the Globe. Flanking the altar, exquisite mosaics depict both apparitions.

Father Skelly's museum of Marian artwork can be viewed in the CAMM offices, located across the street from the shrine.

Come to Mary: 475 East Chelten Avenue, Philadelphia, PA 19144. (800) 523-3674, (215) 848-1010. miraculousmedal.org.

Signs and Wonders

The Blessed Mother showers extraordinary graces and divine protection on wearers of the Miraculous Medal. The following testimonies are excerpted, with permission, from various publications of the Miraculous Medal Shrine in Philadelphia.

• • • • •

My husband was working in an oil tank, half full of oil, when it caught fire. No one knew he was inside. Nor could they have helped him much if they had known, for there was just one small opening into the tank. You can imagine the amazement of the crowd when, after the fire had been extinguished, he crawled out through the small opening, unharmed. He had inhaled some smoke but did not suffer much from that.

My husband always wears a Miraculous Medal, and I have attended the novena services at the Miraculous Medal Shrine for fifteen years. Surely our devotion to the Immaculate Mother of God has well repaid us. We shall be mindful of her goodness all our days. — From testimony published in the 1940s

• • • • •

It was a beautiful night in June 1944 in Holland, where we lived close to the German border. The nights are not always that beautiful, but on this night during World War II, the moon hung low in the sky. Suddenly, the sirens started blaring a scary sound. Mother woke us up and rushed us to the bomb shelter. As we stood on the landing that led down into the shelter, we saw an American Flying Fortress (B-17 bomber) was hit and coming in flames straight at our house. We stood frozen and watched in horror; we knew it could be the end of us and the people around us.

Then, as if someone pushed the plane away from the house in another direction, it fell in a wooded area some distance away. All eight men aboard were killed, and the plane lay in broken pieces over a large area. We were all saved. Three days later, we found a firebomb stuck halfway in the ground a few feet from our house. It had not exploded.

Now the reason we were spared. My mother was a devout Catholic and always prayed to the Blessed Mother. She had nailed a Miraculous Medal way up in the nook of the roof of our house. The Mother of God saved the lives of my family and our neighbors.

I now live in Canada but, even after sixty-one years, I can still remember that frightful night. I did the same thing as my mother and hung a medal above the front and back doors of my own house. I know Our Lady will protect us if we believe in her and pray to her. Also, I wear the Miraculous Medal and the cross of Jesus around my neck on a chain. This is my story. We were saved that night and were freed in September 1944 by American soldiers. — From testimony published in 2013

• • • • •

I would like to share a true story about how a Miraculous Medal saved my life, I mean literally saved my life. I am now a married fifty-year-old father of four children. The story dates back to about 1980 when I was fifteen years old.

I grew up in Mount Airy, not too far from the Miraculous Medal Shrine in Germantown. One afternoon, as my friend, Pete, and I walked along Gowen Avenue over the train track bridge, we found a tape measure by the side of the street that must have fallen off a truck or been left behind by a worker. Being fifteen years old, and having the great ideas that fifteen-year-olds have, we decided it would be a good idea to measure the height of the bridge from Gowen Avenue down to the tracks of the R7 Septa Chestnut Hill East Rail line.

Since I found the tape measure, I insisted to Pete that I should be the one to measure the bridge height. As I fed the metal tape blindly over the five-foot concrete wall, we took turns guessing the height. After about twenty feet of tape disappeared over the edge, there was an immense explosion and a massive bolt of electricity threw me off my feet. That is the last thing I remember. Pete watched as my body convulsed from 12,000 volts of electricity that had entered the tape measure and then my body.

Unbeknownst to us, the tape measure was not going straight down as we had envisioned. Instead, it had ended up laying across both electric lines that power the Septa commuter train. The 12,000 volts traveled up the metal tape measure and entered through my hands and flashed up my arm toward my head.

To this day, Pete swears he saw a bright blue

flash of electricity exit my neck. The electricity did, in fact, exit my body where the chain of the Miraculous Medal I was wearing, which my mother gave me, was touching my skin. It left a visible burn mark on my neck. The inside portion of the bridge over the tracks was partially cracked from the explosion, and the R7 line went down for the afternoon commuters (sorry).

We stumbled back down the block to my house and told my mother what had just happened. She asked if I was okay and proceeded to take me to a doctor. After a medical examination, the doctor told us the Miraculous Medal I was wearing, in fact, had likely saved my life by interrupting and diverting the massive amount of electricity headed directly up my left arm toward my brain.

Miracles do happen! Thank you, Mother Mary, for watching over a couple of dumb fifteen-year-old kids. — From testimony published in 2016

 ## Our Lady of the Miraculous Medal

The ninth of eleven children, St. Catherine Labouré was born May 2, 1806, in a village in Burgundy, France. When Catherine was nine years old, her mother died. Standing on her tippy-toes before a statue of the Blessed Virgin Mary in the family home, the young girl said, "Now, dear Blessed Mother, you will be my mother." In January 1830, Catherine, twenty-three years old, entered the Daughters of

Charity convent in Paris, on Rue du Bac.

(The Daughters of Charity and the Congregation of the Mission are "brother and sister" religious orders. St. Vincent de Paul founded the Congregation of the Mission, known as the Vincentians, in 1625. Eight years later, in 1633, he and St. Louise de Marillac began the Daughters of Charity.)

Around the midnight hour on July 18, 1830, a heavenly child awakened Catherine from her sleep and led her to the convent chapel. The novice watched as a beautiful woman entered the chapel and then sat in the convent director's chair. It was her mother — the Blessed Mother! Catherine knelt at her feet and, resting her hands on the Virgin's knee, conversed with her for two hours.

Four months later, on November 27, 1830, Our Lady again appeared to Catherine. This time Mary was standing on a globe, dazzling rays of light streaming from her outstretched hands. Framing the oval-shaped apparition was the inscription, "O Mary, conceived without sin, pray for us who have recourse to thee."

Catherine then saw on Mary's fingers rings of precious stones, the source of the beaming rays of light. Mary told her the rays symbolize the graces that she bestows to all who ask for them. The stones that shed no light represent the graces that people don't ask for. Our Lady instructed Catherine, "Have a medal struck after this model [the oval apparition]. Those who wear the medal will receive great graces, especially if they wear it around the neck."

The first medals were struck in 1832 and distributed by the Daughters of Charity to the sick and poor in Paris. Miracles and graces began to flow, and word of the Miraculous Medal spread throughout France and later the world. Everyone wanted the medal that Mary had brought from heaven to earth! Only ten of the original medals struck in 1832 are known to exist today. One of them can be found at the Miraculous Medal Shrine in Philadelphia, Pennsylvania.

The feast of Our Lady of the Miraculous Medal is November 27.

DOYLESTOWN

The Christ Child was born in a stable; her shrine in Pennsylvania began in a barn. The Three Kings paid homage to the Child; she welcomes presidents and prime ministers. Who is this lady with mystical ties? Our Lady of Czestochowa at Doylestown! This is only the beginning of her intriguing story.

According to tradition, Our Lady of Czestochowa, also called the Black Madonna, picked the site of her shrine at Jasna Góra (Polish for "Bright Mountain") in southern Poland. In America, her Doylestown shrine is located on Beacon Hill. The Jasna Góra shrine houses the original wonderworking icon of Our Lady, the Doylestown shrine two exact replicas — both touched to the original and blessed by pope-saints. (What are the miracle odds of that?) Both shrines are tended by the Pauline Order.

The American Czestochowa began in 1953, when Fr. Michael Zembrzuski, OSPPE, established the Pauline Order in America and bought forty acres of farmland with living quarters and a small barn. The barn was converted into a chapel and a painting of Our Lady of Czestochowa placed inside. So many pilgrims came to visit Our Lady in the barn chapel that more land and a bigger shrine were needed.

Overlooking Peace Valley in historic Bucks County near Philadelphia, the 170-acre **National Shrine of Our Lady of Czestochowa** was dedicated on October 16, 1966 — the same year as the millennial anniversary of Christianity in Poland. Mary's first presidential pilgrims: President Lyndon B. Johnson, his wife, Lady Bird, and their daughter Lynda. Everyone was Polish and Catholic that day!

Our Lady's Chapel in the lower church is a stunning replica of her shrine in Poland — from the ebony wood altar to the silver artwork to the miraculous painting, blessed and signed in 1980 by Polish Pope St. John Paul II.

But it's the upper church where eyes explode in wonder. Framed by a breathtaking sixty-five-foot-wide wooden bas relief of the Most Holy Trinity (note the enormous trumpet-blowing angels), another replica of Our Lady of Czestochowa — this one blessed by Pope St. John XXIII — hangs on the sanctuary wall. In the nave, two great walls of stained glass present the history of both Poland and the United States. Spanning forty by fifty feet, each stained-glass wall has seventy-five panels.

The Polish window depicts the thousand-year

Christian history of the nation: from a Slavic pagan god to the "Baptism of Poland" and Prince Mieszko I in 966; to the Hussite attack in 1430 on Jasna Góra that caused scars on the Black Madonna's face; to the 1920 Miracle of the Vistula that saved Catholic Poland from Communist Russia.

On the opposite stained-glass wall, panels portray the history of America: from Columbus' historic voyage in 1492; to the founding of the first European settlement at St. Augustine, Florida, in 1565 (see site 12); to the signing of the Declaration of Independence in 1776; to the first Polish settlement at Panna Maria (Polish for "Virgin Mary"), Texas, on Christmas Day, 1854.

A towering statue of Pope John Paul II stands outside the church, his eyes crinkled in delight and arms open wide in greeting. At the base are inscribed his famous Marian words of consecration, *Totus Tuus* ("I'm all yours"). As Cardinal Karol Wojtyla, he visited the shrine twice, in 1969 and 1976. During his 1976 visit, he sent the monastery novices for takeout: He wanted pizza! As Pope John Paul II, he blessed and signed the Black Madonna icon housed in the lower church.

The grounds also hold numerous prayer stations, including St. Anne's Chapel and the Our Lady of the Unborn statue. The popular Polish American Festival is held here on the first two weekends in September.

Come to Mary: 654 Ferry Road, Doylestown, PA 18901. (215) 345-0600. czestochowa.us.

Bas-relief and image of Our Lady of Czestochowa in the upper church — National Shrine of Our Lady of Czestochowa, Doylestown, Pennsylvania

Signs and Wonders

Who can attract the famous and powerful? The Black Madonna at the American Czestochowa in Doylestown! During the shrine's dedication on October 16, 1966, President Lyndon B. Johnson addressed a crowd of some 100,000 spectators. Vice President Hubert H. Humphrey visited in 1967. Future Vice President and President George H. W. Bush delivered a speech here in 1980.

President Ronald Reagan's address during the annual Polish American Festival on September 9, 1984, brought down the church-house. Lauding the beautiful church, the president said, "This shrine with its magnificent stained glass stands out not only as a monument to the heart and soul of Polish America but as a tribute to the cause of human freedom itself." He also praised the love and joy the Polish have for the Black Madonna and her special inspiration to the Holy Father. "Thank God for Pope John Paul II!" President Reagan exclaimed.

A bronze statue of President Reagan, seated at a picnic table with a *placki* (Polish potato pancake) on his plate, commemorates the event.

A Polish soldier, his life spared by a Polish saint, also paid homage to Our Lady of Doylestown. During World War II, Franciszek Gajowniczek, a Polish army sergeant held captive at the Auschwitz concentration camp, was sentenced to die. St. Maximilian Kolbe, OFM Conv, a fellow prisoner, offered to die in his place. Gajowniczek, who later dedicated his life to spreading the story of Father Kolbe's heroic love, visited the American Czestochowa in 1984 and 1987.

Our Lady of Czestochowa

According to tradition, the portrait of Our Lady of Czestochowa was painted by someone who knew the Blessed Mother in person: St. Luke the Evangelist, the Church's first iconographer. Even more intriguing is that the icon was reputed to have been painted "on a board from a table at which the Holy Family prayed and ate their meals in Nazareth," reported Pauline Father Gabriel Lorenc in *American Czestochowa*.

It's said the icon was lost about AD 72, when the Romans sacked Jerusalem. In 326, Saint Helena found the painting in Jerusalem and gave it to her son, Constantine the Great. The emperor enshrined the icon in a church at Constantinople, where it remained for nearly five centuries.

In 803, the Byzantine emperor gave the painting as a wedding gift to a Greek princess who married a Ruthenian nobleman. The icon took up residence in a castle at Belz for five hundred years. When the Tartars attacked Ruthenia in the mid-fourteenth century, Prince Ladislaus of Opole built a monastery for the Pauline Fathers at Czestochowa, in today's southern Poland, and entrusted the miracle painting to them, about 1382.

In 1430, Hussite soldiers attacked the monastery and tried to destroy the icon. One soldier struck the painting with his sword, creating two scars on Our Lady's right cheek. When he raised the sword the third time, he was struck dead. The other soldiers fled, leaving behind the mutilated icon.

Fast forward five hundred years to the Second World War, when many monasteries and cathedrals across Europe were obliterated. It remains a mystery "why the Germans did not bomb Jasna Góra," continued Father Lorenc, "why the Shrine was not closed, why the Pauline seminarians were allowed to remain at Jasna Góra and continue their studies."

More than 12,000 Nazi generals, marshals, and officers visited Jasna Góra and signed the monastic guest books. One visitor was Adolf Hitler himself. Did the Nazis know the story of the Hussite soldier who was struck dead? Were they afraid of destroying Our Lady's shrine and icon and being struck dead themselves? Only heaven knows.

The feast of Our Lady of Czestochowa is August 26.

CENTRALIA

⑦

Reader's Digest called it "the church that wouldn't burn." Others say the **Assumption of the Blessed Virgin Mary Ukrainian Catholic Church** in Centralia, a coal-mining ghost town in the Appalachian Mountains, is a miracle.

"The church shouldn't be there, but every Sunday, parishioner John Mayernick goes anyway," reported Bill Hangley Jr. in 2018 for *Reader's Digest*. "He opens the door that shouldn't be standing, walks past the pews that should have burned, and mounts the stairs to the balcony that should have been razed."

Then he rings the church bells.

Centralia, located 115 miles northwest of Philadelphia, was settled in the mid-1800s by miners of black gold: anthracite coal. Hungarian, Czech, Ukrainian, Polish, and Irish miners all poured into the area, putting down deep roots. Generation after generation of miners descended into the mines to extract the black gold.

In its heyday, Centralia boasted seven churches, two theaters, five hotels, twenty-seven saloons, a bank and a post office, and fourteen general and grocery stores. It was a little immigrant heaven on earth.

Then, in 1962, the town caught fire. No one knows exactly how the fire started, but some speculate it began when trash being burned in the town dump wasn't fully extinguished. The fire ignited a vein of coal beneath the dump and then began feeding on underground coal seams and a labyrinth of old mine tunnels. Slowly, the town began to cave in.

A section of State Highway 61 buckled and

collapsed. Eerie wisps of smoke appeared like ghosts in church cemeteries. On Valentine's Day, 1981, twelve-year-old Todd Domboski was standing in his grandmother's backyard when the earth collapsed under his feet. By a miracle of heaven, he was able to grab a tree root and cling tight until his cousin pulled him out of the sinkhole to safety.

The town also got hot. The owner of a gasoline station recorded an extremely high temperature reading of his underground gas tank. Residents said basement walls were hot to the touch. Snow melted on the "heated sidewalks."

State and federal governments spent millions of dollars to put out the fire. It kept burning, and could burn for 250 more years, experts say. In the 1980s, government officials began buying up properties and relocating residents. Streets were emptied; homes and storefronts razed. St. Ignatius Roman Catholic Church and Protestant churches met the bulldozer. Would the Ukrainian Catholic church be next?

Founded in 1911, the white frame church — with blue onion-shaped domes and three-bar crosses — stood high on a hill overlooking Centralia below. Inside the Byzantine jewel were gilt-framed paintings, an *iconostasis* (a wall of icons that separates the nave from the sanctuary), and a copy of the wonderworking icon of Our Lady of Pochaev. Would Our Lady save her church? In a geological wonder, it was discovered the church wasn't built on a coal seam like the rest of the town, but on solid rock!

Every Sunday, dispersed parishioners drive back to the ghost town and the little miracle church on a hill. They sing. They pray. They give thanks. Assumption of the Blessed Virgin Mary Ukrainian Catholic Church is alive — very much alive!

Come to Mary: North Paxton Street, Centralia, PA 17921. (570) 339-0650. ukrarcheparchy.us /assumption-of-bvm-centralia.

Exterior — Assumption of the Blessed Virgin Mary Ukrainian Catholic Church, Centralia, Pennsylvania

Maryland

8 ▶ EMMITSBURG

Many of Our Lady's apparitions and famous holy sites began with a dazzling light. In 1805, legend goes, Fr. Jean DuBois saw a light on a hill near Emmitsburg. He followed the light to a beautiful place and planted a rude cross in a large hollowed-out tree that resembled a grotto. From these humble beginnings evolved the beautiful **National Shrine Grotto of Our Lady of Lourdes** at Mount St. Mary's University. This is "Mary's land," after all.

On March 25, 1634 — the feast of the Annunciation — the English ships the *Dove* and the *Ark*, carrying both Catholics and Protestants, landed at St. Clements Island in the Potomac River. The settlers named their new colony Maryland after England's Queen Mary. For Catholic colonists, Maryland also honored Mary, Queen of Heaven. The first town was called St. Mary's City and was located on St. Mary's River. Up went the first Catholic church in

English-speaking America.

When religious tolerance in the colony was rescinded a few decades later, persecuted Catholics began pushing westward. In 1728, the William Elder family and other refugees settled some 150 miles northwest in the first range of the Blue Mountains, near the Pennsylvania border. They called the mountain St. Mary's Mount and the valley, St. Joseph's Valley. The Elder farmhouse became known as Elder's Station, where itinerant priests traveling in disguise offered private Masses.

And so it came to pass in Mary's land that Father DuBois, a refugee of the bloody, anti-Catholic French Revolution, followed the light in 1805 and discovered his grotto in a great oak tree in a stream. "With the passing of time, the earth had been washed out from beneath the great, gnarled roots of the oak," noted *The Story of the Grotto*, creating a recess "underneath the great trunk and the thick roots which overhung the bed of the stream. In summer, when the stream was low, one could enter the grotto and find a rustic room."

Father DuBois also built St. Mary's Church (1805) on a hilltop and founded today's Mount St. Mary's University and Seminary (1808) on the slopes below. Both sinner and saint began coming to the hallowed mountain. St. Elizabeth Ann Seton, who founded the Sisters of Charity of St. Joseph at Emmitsburg in 1809, would sit on "her rock" at the grotto to teach the children the catechism. St. John Neumann also walked these wooded paths.

In 1858, Our Lady appeared to Bernadette at Lourdes, France. Less than twenty years later, in 1875, she made an appearance in Emmitsburg in a stone grotto patterned after Lourdes. Adding a spiri-

tual connection to the French shrine, the grotto contains a stone from Lourdes that pilgrims can touch while asking Our Lady's prayers. A plaque at the grotto spring reads, "Let anyone who thirsts come to me and drink ... rivers of living water will flow from within him (John 7:37–38)."

Like the mother grotto, many stupendous healings of body and soul are reported at the daughter shrine. A Baltimore psychiatrist had an operation for an ear condition that resulted in loss of hearing. He applied grotto spring water to his ear and was instantly healed of his deafness. A forty-four-year-old drug addict and alcoholic kicked his addictions after praying here. Seminarians reported being cured of eye afflictions.

Some pilgrims claim to see mystical flashes of light, as though Our Lady is moving in the woods, while others hear heavenly music. On foggy days, other pilgrims feel wrapped in the supernatural, as though the Blessed Mother has descended in a cloud among them. Etched on the grotto ambo are the words, "For those who believe in God, no explanation is necessary; for those who do not believe in God, no explanation is possible."

Watching over Mary's land is the Pangborn Memorial Campanile, added about 1964. Ninety-five-feet tall and visible for miles, the bell tower is crowned with a twenty-five-foot, gold-leafed bronze figure of the Blessed Mother. (Her May Crowning, at 120 feet in the air, is quite a spectacle.) The campanile stands on the hilltop site of Father DuBois' old St. Mary's Church, which burned down in 1913.

Lourdes Grotto — National Shrine Grotto of Our Lady of Lourdes, Emmmitsburg, Maryland

The Corpus Christi Chapel (1905), seating eight, replaced the original tree grotto.

In addition to Our Lady's grotto statue that dates from 1891, Marian figures inhabiting the grounds include Our Lady of La Vang, Mary Help of Christians, Our Lady of Perpetual Help, Our Lady of Grace, Our Lady of Fátima, Virgin of the Poor, Our Lady of Guadalupe, Our Lady of Mount Carmel, Our Lady of Sorrows, and a striking portrayal of the Nativity. Laying on a bed of straw, the Blessed Mother reaches out to touch her newborn Son in the manger.

Come to Mary: 16330 Grotto Road (on the campus of Mount St. Mary's University), Emmitsburg, MD 21727. (301) 447-5318. nsgrotto.org.

Signs and Wonders

When Fr. Jean DuBois founded Mount St. Mary's Seminary and College (now University) at Emmitsburg in 1808, a legendary institution was born. From this holy mountain came many "firsts" in American Catholic history:

- Fr. John Baptist Purcell was named the first bishop (1833) of Cincinnati, Ohio.
- Fr. William J. Quarter, the first bishop (1844) of Chicago, Illinois.
- Fr. Francis X. Gartland, the first bishop (1850) of Savannah, Georgia.
- Fr. John J. Hughes, the first archbishop (1850) of the Archdiocese of New York.
- Fr. Richard V. Whelan, the first bishop (1850) of the Diocese of Wheeling, West Virginia.
- Fr. George A. Carroll, SJ, the first bishop (1853) of Covington, Kentucky.
- Fr. John McCloskey, the first American Cardinal (1875).
- Bl. Stanley Rother, an Oklahoma native and a 1963 graduate of Mount St. Mary's Seminary, met a martyr's death on July 28, 1981, at his mission in Guatemala. The priest is the first American-born martyr to be beatified.

Our Lady of Lourdes

The well-known story of Our Lady of Lourdes began on February 11, 1858. Peasant girl Bernadette Soubirous was collecting firewood at the River Gave, when she heard a peculiar rustling sound and looked up. Standing in a natural grotto was a beautiful young Lady! She was dressed in a white robe, a blue sash around her waist. Her hair was covered with a white veil, and a yellow rose rested on each of her bare feet. Draped on her right arm was a large rosary. Bernadette prayed her rosary and then the Lady disappeared.

That was the first of Our Lady's eighteen apparitions at Lourdes, located in the Pyrenees Mountains in southern France. During the ninth apparition, on February 25, Our Lady told Bernadette to drink from the spring and wash in it. There was no spring, so Bernadette began digging in the dirt. Water began bubbling up, and Bernadette cupped her hands to drink of the water and to wash her face. From that spring flow the healing waters of Lourdes today.

A month later, on March 25 — the feast of the Annunciation — Our Lady revealed her identity to Bernadette. "I am the Immaculate Conception," she said. Bernadette, poor and illiterate, didn't know what that meant. But the learned clergy did and marveled at Bernadette's words. How could this girl know that four years earlier, on December 8, 1854, Pope Pius IX had declared the Immaculate Conception of Mary a dogma of the Catholic Church?

The feast of Our Lady of Lourdes is February 11.

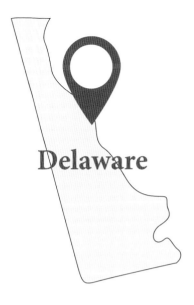

NEW CASTLE

9

You might call it a case of "Mary envy."

In 1982, sculptor Charles C. Parks put on public display in downtown Wilmington, Delaware, his thirty-two-foot stainless steel statue of the Immaculate Heart of Mary. Commissioned by Fr. John J. Sweeney for Our Lady of Peace Church in Santa Clara, California (see site 50), the statue attracts tourists and pilgrims like honey. She's ravishing! In 1998, the renowned artist exhibited another stainless steel wonder: the thirty-three-foot Our Lady of the New Millennium, now installed at St. John, Indiana (see site 23).

Catholics in Delaware were smitten! They wanted their own Parks statue of Mary. Spearheading the monumental effort were the Delaware Knights of Columbus, Marian groups, and parishioners from around the Wilmington diocese. But where to place the novel statue? Bishop Michael A. Saltarelli decided to make Mega Mary visible to the masses: She would reside on the grounds of Holy Spirit Church in New Castle — in clear view of motorists traveling Interstate 295.

Like Father Sweeney's flock in California, lo-

cal Catholics began praying in the money and filled out "rosary checks," payable to Our Lady, to record the number of Rosaries prayed. Their goal: 500,000 Rosaries to raise the $500,000 cost of the statue. The rosary checks topped 500,000 Rosaries — and donations began pouring in before any formal fundraising was launched.

Our Lady Queen of Peace stands thirty-three-feet tall and weighs four tons, her welcoming arms and Immaculate Heart imitating the California statue. Her face, however, is the likeness of Mary's image at Medjugorje. At times, Mega Mary glows like an apparition on the horizon. Her mantle and gown of welded strips of stainless steel reflect a silvery aura during the day; at dawn and dusk, a celestial gold. And who wouldn't fall for her in the shimmering light of the moon?

Dedicated on May 26, 2007, the **Shrine of Our Lady Queen of Peace** is a heavenly welcome sign of sorts to the multitudes of commuters who cross the Delaware Memorial Bridge from New Jersey into northeastern Delaware. Many travelers tuck written prayers and mementos into the folds of her gown, while other pilgrims revel in the beauty of her presence. To everyone she is a miracle — a miracle wrought by the power of the Rosary.

Come to Mary: 12 Winder Road (GPS: 6 Church Drive), New Castle, DE 19720. (302) 658-1069. https://www.holyspiritchurchde.org/our-lady -queen-of-peace-statue.html.

Shrine of Our Lady Queen of Peace — Holy Spirit Church, New Castle, Delaware

SOUTHEAST

Fort Smith

Memphis

Little Rock

Birmingham

Shreveport

Meridian

Jackson

Baton Rouge

Mobile

Biloxi

New Orleans

Gulf of Mexico

BELMONT

10

When the New Eve, an ancient title for Mary, inhabits a place, all things are made new — even a slave auction block. That's the legacy of **Abbey Basilica of Mary Help of Christians of Belmont Abbey and Belmont Abbey College**, in the small western North Carolina town of Belmont.

When Benedictine monks settled here in 1876, they named the priory Mariastein (German for "Mary's Rock") in honor of the Blessed Virgin Mary and for a large granite boulder on the property. Tradition holds the rock was once used by the Catawba Indians as a ceremonial stone and later by white men to auction off slaves. With time, the rock was buried and forgotten.

In the 1960s, the old slave stone was unearthed,

Baptismal font made from former slave auction block — Abbey Basilica of Mary Help of Christians, Belmont, North Carolina

made into a baptismal font, and placed inside the Abbey Basilica. A brass legend reads, "Upon this rock, men once were sold into slavery. Now upon this rock, through the waters of Baptism, men become free children of God." The stone wasn't the only thing made new — so are souls. The baptismal waters hold the miracle of eternal life.

A grotto tells another miracle story. In June 1890, Fr. Francis Meyer, OSB, a young abbey priest, contracted the deadly typhoid fever. Despite the monks' fervent prayers, Father Meyer's health deteriorated. Everyone was afraid he would die. Fr. Felix Hintemeyer, monastery prior, appended their prayers with a promise: If the priest lived, the monks would build a grotto to Our Lady of Lourdes.

Father Meyer sprang back to health, and the monks went forth to haul in granite boulders to construct the grotto. The Grotto of Our Lady of Lourdes was blessed on May 7, 1891, as the "Southern shrine of the Queen of the Clergy for Priestly Vocations."

Appearing in a niche is a larger-than-life statue of Our Lady. An adjoining cave houses an altar.

Like Lourdes, the Belmont grotto held a spring. It also had a creek, a "favorite habitat of the copperheads," reported Dom Paschal Baumstein, OSB, in *My Lord of Belmont*. "When someone was bitten, the brothers would stick the afflicted limb inside the carcass of a chicken to draw out the poison. No deaths were recorded."

Completed in 1894, the Abbey Basilica of Mary Help of Christians is known for its prize-winning windows of saints, exhibited at the Chicago's World Fair in 1893. Designed as gothic arches, the eighteen-foot-tall windows aren't stained glass but portraits painted on glass. Look closely and you'll notice different artistic styles. That's because different artists painted the windows, explained Dom Paschal. "The renaissance styling in the hands of Saint Maurus contrasted with the gloved, quasi-Byzantine effect of Saint Anselm." Saint Placid's powerful and provocative face is "set off by an undetailed cloak that seemed almost unfinished."

A historic statue of Mary Help of Christians stands high in the sanctuary, a reminder to always look up in times of need.

Come to Mary: 100 Belmont Mount Holly Road, Belmont, NC 28012. (704) 461-6675. belmontabbey .org.

Georgia

ATLANTA

Mother Mary has her "men" everywhere. Nobody knows this better than parishioners of the **Catholic Shrine of the Immaculate Conception** in Atlanta. Fr. Thomas O'Reilly was her "man" during the American Civil War, and Fr. Joseph R. Smith during World War II.

The fascinating tale of Our Lady's men begins in the fall of 1864, when Union Major General William Tecumseh Sherman began his March to the Sea, burning everything — fields, villages, bridges — in its path. His scorched-earth policy was intended to break the Confederacy's back and thereby end the War Between the States. But Sherman wasn't expecting the likes of Father O'Reilly, pastor of Immaculate Conception Church in Atlanta and a Confederate chaplain tending to wounded Union and Confederate soldiers alike. The thirty-three-year-old upstart cleric heard confessions, performed last rites, and wrote letters to soldiers' kin back home.

"He knew no distinction between the men wearing the blue or those clad in tattered uniform of gray," wrote Van Buren Colley, a noted Atlanta photographer and a member of the Shrine parish, in *History of the Diocesan Shrine of the Immaculate Conception*. "All were children of God in need of help."

When the feisty priest, born in County Cavan, Ireland, learned of Sherman's plan to burn Atlanta to the ground, he stood up to the major general like David to Goliath. Instead of stones, Father O'Reilly hurled fiery words at Sherman — words relayed by General Henry W. Slocum, Sherman's Union commander in Atlanta. Nobody was going to destroy Our Lady's church!

"If you burn Immaculate Conception Church, every Catholic Union soldier in Atlanta will mutiny," Father O'Reilly warned Sherman. And if the Union soldiers didn't mutiny, legend holds, Father O'Reilly vowed to excommunicate them on the spot. Sherman, who had a Catholic upbringing and knew his Atlanta forces were mostly Irish Catholic immigrants, spared the 1848 wooden church.

(According to historical accounts, Sherman was baptized in the Presbyterian faith of his birth family and entered into the Catholic Faith with his foster family. He reportedly stopped attending church during the Civil War. His wife, Ellen Ewing Sherman, was devoutly Catholic, and the couple's eight children were raised Catholic. His son, Thomas, became a Jesuit priest and presided at his funeral Mass in 1891. Sherman rests in Calvary Cemetery, a Catholic

The Immaculate Conception, Bartolome Esteban Murillo, c. 1674

cemetery, in St. Louis, Missouri.)

Father O'Reilly also interceded for Atlanta's city hall and courthouse and for four Protestant churches, all within the immediate vicinity of the Catholic church. The churches were spared destruction, but not Union occupation. Union troops took command of St. Philip's Episcopal Church "as a stable for their horses," continued Colley, "the basement of Central Presbyterian was used as a slaughterhouse for hogs to feed [Sherman's] Army; the Trinity Methodist was protected as a storehouse for furniture of the prosperous citizens evacuating the city."

Immaculate Conception Church — Atlanta's first Catholic church — served as a makeshift hospital, its floorboards permanently stained with blood. Second Baptist Church, the only church left suitable for worship, held Christmas services in 1864. Guards were posted around the churches and a buffer zone of houses created to control "the burning of Atlanta." As a result, four hundred homes were also spared.

The war over, in 1869 Father O'Reilly began building the Gothic-inspired Catholic Shrine of the Immaculate Conception. He died in 1872, at age forty-one, his health weakened from both the war and the effects of yellow fever suffered years earlier. His mortal remains rest in a crypt under the church sanctuary.

In 1945, the Atlanta Historical Society honored the gallant priest with a monument on the grounds of the nearby Atlanta City Courthouse.

During World War II, Our Lady raised up another holy man: Fr. Joseph R. Smith. A Catholic convert, Father Smith watched in agony as parishioner-soldiers left to fight. He not only urged his congregants to offer their Masses and Communions for their men at war, but he initiated the public recitation of the Rosary at Masses for their safe return. Not one parishioner died in the conflict. Father Smith credited the feat to Our Lady's miraculous intercession. (See St. Benedict, Kansas, site 38; St. Marks, Kansas, site 39; Leopold, Missouri, site 35; Arapahoe, Nebraska, site 36; and Windthorst, Texas, site 45.)

The shrine is lauded for its signature stained-glass window *The Immaculate Conception*, patterned after one of Bartolomé Esteban Murillo's seventeenth-century paintings. Like soldiers in the Army of God, life-size frescoes of the Apostles line the nave ceiling.

Come to Mary: 48 Martin Luther King Jr. Drive SW, Atlanta, GA 30303. (404) 521-1866. catholicshrineatlanta.org.

Signs and Wonders

What happened to the four Protestant churches in Atlanta saved by Fr. Thomas O'Reilly in 1864? Surprisingly, all four congregations remain active today.

Established in 1846 with five communicants, St. Philip's Episcopal Church was used as a horse stable by Union forces during the siege of Atlanta. The present church, in the Buckhead neighborhood, serves as the Cathedral of St. Philip for the Episcopal Diocese of Atlanta.

The Union army commandeered Central Presbyterian Church as a slaughterhouse. Unlike many downtown Protestant churches that moved to the suburbs, Central Presbyterian remained where it was planted and is dubbed "The Church That Stayed."

Trinity Methodist Church, Atlanta's first brick church, served as a warehouse for residents to store their belongings before fleeing the burning of Atlanta. In 1911, the congregation moved to its third (and current) church, a short distance from its original location.

Founded in 1854, Second Baptist Church was the only church suitable for Christmas services in 1864. The congregation merged with other Baptist churches and is known today as Second-Ponce de Leon Baptist Church, also located in Buckhead.

Immaculate Conception

Long before December 8, 1854, when Pope Pius IX declared the Immaculate Conception of the Virgin Mary a dogma of the Catholic Church, America was honoring Mary Immaculate.

One of her earliest chapels was the Convento de Immaculada Concepción, about 1573, built by Spanish Franciscans at St. Augustine, Florida (see site 12).

The country's oldest surviving Marian statue came to Santa Fe, New Mexico, in 1626, and resides at the Cathedral Basilica of St. Francis of Assisi (see site 47). One of her early titles was the Immaculate Conception.

Before Fr. Jacques Marquette, French Jesuit missionary and explorer, and Louis Jolliet began their epic canoe ride down the Mississippi in 1673, the priest placed the voyage under the protection of the Immaculate Conception and called the river Conception River.

In 1792, Bishop John Carroll, SJ, the first bishop and later archbishop of the United States, consecrated the fledgling nation to the Immaculate Conception.

In 1846, American bishops chose the Blessed Mother, under the title of Immaculate Conception, as patroness of our country.

Florida

12 ST. AUGUSTINE

"It's a boy!" "It's a girl!" The heaven-sent news often heard at the **National Shrine of Our Lady of La Leche at Mission Nombre de Dios** in St. Augustine, on Florida's northeast coast. Many couples wanting to conceive come here to pray before a statue of Mary nursing the Holy Infant. Nine months later, they're cuddling their own baby. Some are doubly blessed — they have twins!

It's no coincidence the shrine is a powerhouse of answered baby prayers: The city of St. Augustine is "birthed" in firsts. On September 8, 1565, the feast of the Nativity of the Blessed Virgin Mary, Admiral Pedro Menéndez de Avilés and Spanish colonists aboard a fleet of ships came ashore, and Fr. Francisco López de Mendoza Grajales offered the first parish Mass at a permanent settlement in today's United States. (America's first parish is known today as the Cathedral Basilica of St. Augustine.)

Mary's birthday Mass also marked St. Augustine as the birthplace of Christianity in America — fifty-five years before the Puritans landed in 1620 at Plymouth Rock. After the first Mass, the colonists, numbering around eight hundred, and the Timucua Indians shared a meal — the real First Thanksgiving feast, many historians claim.

The mission site where the colonists landed, built a fort, and celebrated the first Mass was "given the name Nombre de Dios, or 'Name of God,'" explained Matthew J. Geiger in the booklet *Mission of Nombre de Dios.* Franciscan missionaries would later use Mission Nombre de Dios as their headquarters, establishing a chain of missions "as far north as the Chesapeake Bay, as far south as Miami, and as far west as Pensacola."

In the early 1600s, the colonists enshrined a small wooden statue of the nursing Madonna in the mission chapel and renamed the chapel Nuestra Señora de la Leche y Buen Parto ("Our Lady of the Milk and Happy Delivery"). The mission that birthed Christianity in America on the feast of Mary's Nativity in 1565 also birthed the country's first Marian shrine. (The nation's oldest Marian statue resides in the Cathedral Basilica of St. Francis of Assisi in Santa Fe, New Mexico. See site 47.)

As the centuries passed, the chapel was rebuilt several times and the original image replaced. Occupying the place of honor in the ivy-draped Historic Chapel, as it's called, is a forty-two-inch statue of Our Lady of La Leche. Canonically crowned on October 10, 2021 — a solemn coronation approved by the pope in honor of an icon's extraordinary graces and devotion (see New Orleans, Louisiana, site 15) — the Blessed Mother is seated on a throne, barefooted, her right foot resting on a pillow. At her breast is the Infant Jesus. As babies do, his right hand clutches the fabric of his Mother's red dress with starry blue mantle.

And that, pilgrims say, is the special allure of Our Lady of La Leche: Like an earthly mother, the Queen of Heaven is nursing her Child. And who knows bet-

ter than the Blessed Mother that every baby is a miracle of God? But sometimes that hoped-for miracle needs a little push — the intercession of Our Lady of La Leche.

Dubbed America's Most Sacred Acre, the old mission site is also lauded for its New Shrine (a larger church where Masses are said); the 208-foot-tall Great Cross of stainless steel; a rustic outdoor altar memorializing the first Mass; and the larger-than-life bronze statue of Father López, his head and arms raised to heaven — all commemorating the birthplace of Christianity in America and the country's first shrine to the Mother of God.

There's more. In 2015, the shrine birthed her first daughter shrine: the Santa Fe Shrine of Our Lady of La Leche in High Springs, Florida (santafeshrineourladylaleche.com).

Come to Mary: 101 San Marco Avenue, St. Augustine, FL 32084. (904) 824-2809. missionandshrine .org.

Historic Chapel — National Shrine of Our Lady of La Leche, St. Augustine, Florida

Signs and Wonders

Only heaven knows the number of babies conceived in prayer at the National Shrine of Our Lady of La Leche in St. Augustine. Newly married couples come in wedding gowns and tuxedos to ask for the gift of a child. Others visit the shrine as proof that Our Lady "delivers." "My mother wanted a baby but couldn't, so she came to the chapel to pray, and here I am," they quip. Still other pilgrims ask for divine help with problem pregnancies and carrying their babies to full term.

• • • • •

Some hopeful parents experience a miracle of the heart. One couple from Louisiana, who made the pilgrimage to pray for a family, found the grace and courage to accept God's will. They decided if they couldn't have a child of their own, they would adopt. And adopt they did — they became parents to nine and grandparents to twenty!

• • • • •

When Anthony and Lisa Smrek first visited the shrine in 1996, they had already experienced a miracle — their unborn baby was still alive. Doctors had diagnosed Lisa with a tubal pregnancy and advised her to terminate the pregnancy. But a chance encounter with a nurse named Maria inspired the couple to wait. A subsequent medical visit confirmed it was not a tubal pregnancy. Daughter Dana was born perfect in every way.

If every baby is a miracle, the Smreks wanted

another. Four years later, in October 2000, they again visited Our Lady's shrine. This time they asked for a "special delivery."

"I had medical procedures and surgery, but I couldn't get pregnant," Lisa, a registered nurse, told Marion Amberg in a *St. Anthony Messenger* article. "I remember thinking, *I'm a good Catholic girl. My husband and I love each other. Everyone else is having babies. Why can't I have another baby?*"

The couple prayed their hearts out before a statue of Our Lady of La Leche. Several weeks later, Lisa felt nudged to do a home pregnancy test. "It was positive," continued Lisa. "I did another test, then another. They were all positive!"

Nine months later, their son, David, was born — an express delivery through prayer. His conception was traced to the time of their pilgrimage to St. Augustine.

Our Lady of La Leche

Devotion to Our Lady of La Leche (Our Lady of the Milk) is nearly two millennia old. According to tradition, the Holy Family was fleeing to Egypt during Herod's Slaughter of the Innocents and stopped in a Bethlehem cave so the Blessed Mother could nurse her Child. As the Child was nursing, a few drops of Mary's milk spilled to the ground and turned the dark stones a chalky white. Miracles were soon attributed to the cave, and around AD 385 the first structure was built over the hallowed site.

The cave is known today as the Milk Grotto

and tended by the Franciscans of the Holy Land. Women of all faiths — Christian, Muslim, and others — come here, seeking Our Lady of the Milk's help with infertility issues and problem pregnancies.

The piety eventually made its way to Spain. In 1598, the story goes, a Spanish noble rescued a small statue of the nursing Mother from a drunken sailor and took it home. The noble's pregnant wife, suffering from an illness that threatened her life and that of her unborn child, invoked Our Lady's intercession. The baby was born healthy, and both lives were spared.

News of the miracle statue spread, and King Philip III erected an ornate chapel for the image in Madrid. (Both chapel and statue were destroyed during the Spanish Civil War.) Many happy deliveries were attributed to Our Lady's intercession. It's said that even "the queen of Spain was among the throngs of expectant mothers to visit the statue," stated Matthew J. Geiger in *Mission Nombre de Dios*. A few years later, a "replica was brought to St. Augustine, and the devotion was reborn in the New World."

Our Lady has been delivering miracle babies here ever since.

The Diocese of St. Augustine celebrates the feast of Our Lady of La Leche on October 11, a diocesan feast approved by the Vatican in 2012.

MIAMI

13

You never know how or when Our Lady will appear. In 1612, three Cubans were in a skiff off the coast of Cuba and got caught in a wicked storm. The trio began praying for their very lives. When the seas calmed, they spotted something bobbing in the water. It was a statue of the Virgin Mary and Child floating — bone dry — on a tablet! Inscribed at the bottom were the Spanish words, "Yo soy la Virgen de la Caridad" ("I am the Virgin of Charity").

The Virgen would become the Cubans' symbol of hope. African slaves looked to her for emancipation. Freedom fighters invoked her help during the Cuban War of Independence from Spain in the late 1800s. The Virgen went underground with them when communist dictator Fidel Castro rose to power in 1959 and seized and desecrated churches. Tens of thousands of Cubans began fleeing the island, many to South Florida.

The Virgen — or Cachita, her endearing nickname — didn't forget her exiled people. Nearly 350 years after she appeared to the three Cubans at sea, she surfaced in Miami, Florida. On September 8, 1961 — the double feasts of the Nativity of the Blessed Virgin Mary and of La Virgen de la Caridad — a crowd of 30,000 exiled Cubans were gathered in a Miami stadium for Mass to pray for Castro's ouster and the safety of relatives back home. Suddenly, Cachita entered the stadium! Surrounded by flowers and carried high on a litter, the sixteen-inch replica statue had been smuggled out of Cuba that very morning. The crowds went wild with ecstasy!

"*¡Milagro!*" the exiles cheered. "It's a miracle!"

In 1967, the Cuban exiles began erecting a sanctuary for Cachita in the Coconut Grove area of Miami. Like the widow's mite, they gave what little they had: pennies. Sacks and sacks of pennies. So many sacks of pennies that priests made daily runs to the bank. **The National Shrine of Our Lady of Charity** (La Ermita de la Caridad) was dedicated on December 2, 1973.

Located on the Bay of Biscayne and pointing to Cuba, the ninety-foot-tall shrine is strikingly unique in design: The conical shape imitates the mantle of Our Lady's statue — the protective mantle of the Holy Mother of God. Under her mantle, on the facade above the main entrance, is a tile mosaic of the three Cubans in their storm-tossed boat.

Inside, the "exiled Virgen," attired in exquisite robes, adorns a 747-square-foot mural portraying

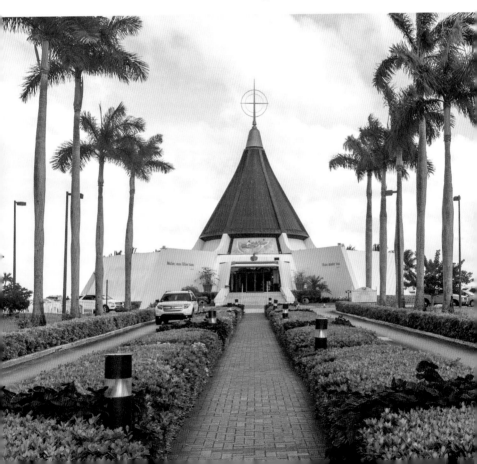

Cuba's long Catholic history. In the adoration chapel, a stained-glass Virgen walks on water. On sunny, breezy days, the reflection of the waves in the bay makes the stained-glass waves move under her feet, observed Maria Morera Johnson, a Cuban exile, in *Our Lady of Charity*. It's as though Cachita is coming to rescue you, just like she did the Cuban boaters in 1612.

Yellow is the traditional color of La Virgen de la Caridad, and the shrine is abloom in yellow roses, yellow daises, and golden sunflowers. Not only do pilgrims bring yellow flowers to Cachita, they often wear yellow clothes. In Christian symbolism, yellow represents hope and joy and the presence of God — the very message of the shrine itself. No matter the storms in life, the Virgen and Child are always there, sometimes in very miraculous ways.

Come to Mary: 3609 South Miami Avenue, Miami, FL 33133. (305) 854-2404, (305) 854-2405. ermita .org.

Exterior — National Shrine of Our Lady of Charity
(Ermita de la Caridad), Miami, Florida

Signs and Wonders

When you love your mother, you won't leave her behind — even if you have to smuggle her to freedom. That's the story of La Virgen de la Caridad at the National Shrine of Our Lady of Charity in Miami.

In the summer of 1961, Fr. Armando Jiménez Rebollar, one of many exiled Cuban priests in Florida, asked his mother in Cuba to send him the replica statue of the Virgen that he had commissioned for his parish church in Guanabo, near Havana. Thus began Our Lady's international smuggling ring.

The sixteen-inch icon was secreted "from a carpenter's workshop to a private Havana house to the Italian Embassy to the Panamanian Embassy," reported Lizette Alvarez in the *New York Times*. The final hand-off was to a Cuban political refugee who had been granted asylum in the United States. Toting the statue in a blue bag, the refugee boarded a flight for Miami and carried Cuba's patron saint to freedom.

La Virgen de la Caridad has been Queen of Miami ever since.

Our Lady of Charity

The legend of Nuestra Señora de la Caridad, Our Lady of Charity, dates from 1612, when two Indian brothers Rodrigo and Juan de Hoyos and African slave boy Juan Moreno were in a rowboat on the Bay of Nipe, off eastern Cuba. They were out harvesting salt for a slaughterhouse in Barajagua, which needed the salt to preserve the meat supply for the copper miners and their families in El Cobre ("Copper"). A fierce storm blew in and began rocking the boat.

The trio invoked Our Lady's protection. The waters calmed and the skies cleared. In the distance, they saw something bobbing in the water. They began rowing toward the object, as the waves carried it to them. It was a small statue of Mary and Child lashed to a board! Mary held the Child Jesus in her left arm, a gold cross in her raised right hand. On the board were written the Spanish words, "Yo soy la Virgen de la Caridad" ("I am the Virgin of Charity"). Much to their amazement, the water-borne statue was inexplicably dry.

The "Three Juans," as the trio came to be called, took the statue to the village of Barajagua, where a small chapel was built in her honor. One night, Rodrigo went to visit the Virgen, but she was gone! How could this be? The chapel had been locked. The next morning, the statue was back in her chapel — wet, as though it had traveled on water.

When this happened three times, one account has it, the villagers of Barajagua decided the Virgen wanted to be in a different location, so they took her to a church in El Cobre. But the Virgen's disappearing act continued! One day, a young girl was chasing butterflies and picking wildflowers in the nearby mountains, when she found the statue on a hilltop. A church was erected for Our Lady on that hallowed spot, and she began working many miracles there.

Today's National Shrine Basilica of Our Lady

of Charity of El Cobre, with its flight of 254 steps, was dedicated in 1926.

Often called the Cuban Lourdes, the basilica tells yet another story — the tale of Ernest Hemingway's *The Old Man and the Sea*. The famous novel centers on Santiago, an old Cuban fisherman after the "big one," a giant marlin. Santiago vows to make a pilgrimage to the Virgen of El Cobre if he catches the fish. He does.

The book won Hemingway the 1954 Nobel Prize in Literature. Honoring Santiago's promise, Hemingway made the pilgrimage to El Cobre, near Santiago de Cuba, and gave the Nobel Prize medal to Our Lady's basilica, where it remains to this day.

The feast of Our Lady of Charity is September 8.

KEY WEST

With faith like a grain of mustard seed, you can move mountains — or stop hurricanes. That's the forecast of Our Lady of Lourdes Grotto on the grounds of the **Basilica of Saint Mary Star of the Sea** in Key West. When hurricanes threaten Key West, the southernmost populated island in the Florida Keys, national and local television crews broadcast from the "hurricane grotto."

"Will Mary stop another hurricane?" the newscasters ask, unwittingly propagating the century-old story of Our Lady and a nun.

When Sr. M. Louis Gabriel, SNJM, arrived in Key West on August 25, 1897, she was eighteen years old and had taken vows only three weeks earlier. The young teaching sister heard tales of the Great Hurricane of 1846, which took out lighthouses and all but eight of 600 homes in Key West, and of the "twin hurricanes" in 1870, nine days apart. Before long, she had her own 'cane stories.

On October 17, 1906, Sister Gabriel survived her first major hurricane; some two hundred Key West residents did not. Three years later, on October 11, 1909, another hurricane battered the island. Hundreds of buildings collapsed or were swept away. On September 10, 1919, a category 4 hurricane severely damaged nearly every home and business in Key West and sank the steamer *Valbanera*. All 488 passengers perished, their bodies lost at sea.

Enough was enough! Sister Gabriel turned her sights — and the sights of the Key West natives, or Conchs — to the "Eye" above. "With her twenty-fifth anniversary as a religious coming up, she was offered a trip to Rome" to mark the event, reported Marcy Knight in *Florida Catholic*. "Instead, she asked to build a replica of Our Lady of Lourdes" grotto in France on the grounds of Saint Mary Star of the Sea Church.

Sister Gabriel designed the enormously tall shrine, and the Conchs collected coral rock from around the island to build it. Standing in an alcove in the craggy grotto is Our Lady of Lourdes statue, a Bernadette statue kneeling on a stone pedestal below. Pilgrims cozy up to Bernadette and gaze up at Our Lady — just like the peasant girl did during Our Lady's visits to her in 1858. A path of inlaid stones, replicating a rosary, leads to the grotto.

During the grotto dedication on May 25, 1922, Sister Gabriel prophesied, "As long as the Grotto stands, Key West will never again experience the full brunt of a hurricane." As the Conchs are quick to attest, there hasn't been a deadly hurricane on the island since! During hurricane season, they light candles at the grotto and pray down heaven's protection. According to lore, one man said, "I don't believe in God, but I do believe in the grotto!"

A bust of Sister Gabriel and her prophetic prayer are found on the grotto grounds.

Decades before Sister Gabriel and the islanders erected the now famous shrine, Our Lady was already manifesting her presence in Key West. When a 1901 fire destroyed the first church, erected about 1851, the only item not badly burned was a painted plaque of Mary Star of the Sea.

Mary's Star rose again in 1904 as today's Basilica of Saint Mary Star of the Sea. An eclectic blend of American Victorian architecture, the airy interior

Stained-glass window of Mary, Star of the Sea — Basilica of Saint Mary Star of the Sea, Key West, Florida

imparts the feeling of sailing on celestial seas. Tall louvered doors in the nave let in tropical breezes; the colored glass "porthole" windows above the doors, beams of light. At the helm, over the altar, is a stained-glass window of Mary Star of the Sea, her Child anchored in her arms.

Come to Mary: 1010 Windsor Lane, Key West, FL 33040. (305) 294-1018. stmarykeywest.com.

Signs and Wonders

The Grotto versus the hurricanes. Who's winning? Has Key West suffered the full brunt of a hurricane since Our Lady of Lourdes Grotto was dedicated on May 25, 1922? A staggering loss of life? The utter destruction of island homes and businesses? According to Marcy Knight's 2013 story in *Florida Catholic* titled "Deliver us from storms," the grotto appears to be doing just that:

"On September 2, 1935, the Labor Day hurricane struck Upper Matecumbe Key. More than 200 Florida East Coast Railway workers were killed. Key West had minor damage.

"On September 13, 1948, Sister Gabriel died. Eight days later, Key West felt the western eye wall of a category 3 hurricane. Two weeks later, on October 5, 1948, 'Hurricane 8' came ashore at Key West with winds estimated at 100 miles per hour. Both times, Key West had minor damage.

"The middle keys were hit by Hurricane Donna on September 9, 1960; Key West sustained minor damage.

"Hurricane Betsy hit the upper keys on September 8, 1965; minor damage was reported in Key West.

"Hurricane Floyd hit the lower keys on October 12, 1987. The overall damage amounted to around $500,000 (in 1987 dollars). No casualties or injuries were reported.

"Hurricane Georges hit Key West on September 25, 1998. The storm overturned two boats, caused some damage to over 1,000 homes, and destroyed a large number of mobile homes. There was no loss of life.

"Hurricane Wilma in 2005 caused several feet of water in the low-lying areas, and sixty percent of homes reported flood damage."

Who's winning, Our Lady or the hurricanes? Our Lady, of course!

Mary Star of the Sea

The ancient title Stella Maris, or Mary Star of the Sea, didn't begin as a star but rather as a drop in the ocean. In the fifth century, the legend runs, Saint Jerome translated Mary's Hebrew name Miryam, meaning a drop of the sea, to Stilla Maris in Latin. Somehow, perhaps in a scribal error, Stilla became Stella, and Mary went from a drop in the ocean to being the Star of the Sea.

Invoked by seafarers (see Cheektowaga, New York, site 2) and fishermen, Stella Maris is also called upon to calm the stormy seas of everyday life, lest we spiritually capsize and run aground. During the middle ages, the name Stella Maris was conferred upon Polaris, the North Star, because of its role as a navigational guide — just like Mary herself.

The feast of Mary Star of the Sea is September 27.

NEW ORLEANS

Our Lady of Prompt Succor lives up to her name. When you call upon her in times of trouble, she delivers — and fast! (Prompt Succor means "quick help.") Our Lady's prompt succor is legendary in New Orleans, where she worked not one but two bona fide miracles and boasts two miracle statues. Even General Andrew Jackson, a Protestant who would serve two terms as president of the United States, was amazed at her swift intercessory powers.

The first miracle story takes place on Good Friday 1788, when terror struck the Crescent City. The French Quarter was on fire! Driven by strong winds, the Great New Orleans Fire was within sight of the Ursuline Convent and school for girls (now the **Old Ursuline Convent Museum**), when the mother superior raced through the corridors ordering everyone to evacuate lest they perish in the blaze.

At that very moment, an Ursuline sister placed a

small plaster statue of Our Lady and Child — later dubbed the Sweetheart Statue — in a window facing the inferno. Falling on her knees, she prayed, "Our Lady, we are lost unless you hasten to save us." Incredibly, the wind shifted, and the fire turned on itself and burned out.

The Great New Orleans Fire destroyed 850 buildings, but Our Lady's expeditious succor spared the Ursuline Convent and the Historic French Quarter from total ruin. She saved the convent again in 1794, when another great fire took 210 more buildings.

Our Lady's fame spread far and near. When devotees told Mother Ste. Benoit about Mary's rapid response time to prayer, she would reply, "Oh, Our Lady is such a Sweetheart!" The name stuck. Sweetheart's help continued down through the ages. Before leaving to fight in World War II, Airman Albert Richard took pictures of Sweetheart to protect him in battle. After the war, the pilot returned to thank Sweetheart and left his silver wings at her feet.

But it's the Battle of New Orleans that elevated Our Lady to heroine status. A bit of history to set the miracle stage: On June 18, 1812, President James Madison declared war on Great Britain. Known as the War of 1812, the war is also called America's "second war of independence." The British responded by invading and plundering coastal areas, and torching the White House and the US Capitol building on August 24, 1814.

That December, a fleet of British ships with ten thousand Redcoats dropped anchor off the Louisiana coast. Their aim: gain control of the Mississippi

Life-size statue of Our Lady of Prompt Succor — National Votive Shrine of Our Lady of Prompt Succor, New Orleans, Louisiana

River, an essential trade route. It was said that who-
ever ruled the river would rule the country. As the
British plotted their attack, General Jackson and his
ragtag army of three thousand "soldiers" — Tennes-
see and Kentucky backwoodsmen, farmers, blacks
and Indians, even pirates — were widening a canal
on the Chalmette Plain near New Orleans, and using the dirt to erect a tall earthwork fortified with
timber. The British would have to cross a swamp and
climb the parapet to attack the Americans.

Meanwhile, the Ursuline sisters, the women of
New Orleans, and men too old to bear arms were
holding all-night prayer vigils before a life-size stat-

ue of Our Lady of Prompt Succor that had come from France in 1810. "Our Lady, save us from the British!" they cried.

On January 7, 1815, General Jackson learned the battle was being planned for that night. He warned the Ursulines and implored everyone to keep hounding heaven. According to the annals of the Ursuline convent, "the night of January 7 was spent in prayer before the Blessed Sacrament … our Chapel was continuously thronged with pious ladies … all weeping and praying at the feet of the beautiful statue of Our Lady of Prompt Succor." Mother Ste. Marie Olivier de Vézin boldly promised Our Lady to have a Mass of thanksgiving sung in her honor every year should the Americans win.

Fog covered the battlefield at daybreak on Sunday, January 8, as Fr. Louis DuBourg, PSS, began Mass at the Ursuline Convent. On the Chalmette Plain, the British began crossing the swamp. But the British made a tactical mistake: They forgot to bring ladders and couldn't climb the parapet. Meanwhile, one story has it, a breeze blew in and lifted the fog, allowing General Jackson to spot the approaching Redcoats. Was the breeze from Our Lady's robes as she rushed in to answer the people's prayers? Jackson gave the command for his troops to fire.

Back at the Ursuline chapel, a courier ran in during Mass at Communion time and announced, "Victory is ours!" The Battle of New Orleans had lasted less than thirty minutes!

"Divine interposition!" General Jackson told his troops. "While, by the blessing of Heaven, directing the valor of the troops under my command, one of the most brilliant victories in the annals of the war was obtained!"

The general later visited the Ursuline sisters to personally thank them for their days and nights of prayer and asked Father DuBourg to offer a public service of thanksgiving for the "great assistance we have received from the Ruler of All Events."

On January 8, 2015, the annual Solemn Mass of Thanksgiving in honor of Our Lady of Prompt Succor was offered for the 200th time — just as the mother superior had promised. Among the dignitaries in attendance: members of the British Royal Navy.

Both miracle statues can be venerated at the **National Votive Shrine of Our Lady of Prompt Succor**, a double chapel attached to the "new" Ursuline convent and academy, built in the 1920s. Before Vatican II, the Ursuline sisters lived as a cloistered community. The sisters worshiped in the convent chapel, the public in the chapel facing State Street.

Unique Marian stained-glass windows in the convent chapel include the birth of Mary with parents Anne and Joachim and the Presentation of Mary. In the public chapel, stained glass depicts Mary receiving Communion, as well as Our Lady of Prompt Succor.

Come to Mary: 2701 State Street, New Orleans, LA 70118. (504) 473-6750, (504) 866-0200. shrineolps.com.

Old Ursuline Convent Museum: 1112 Chartres Street, New Orleans LA, 70116. (504) 529-3040. stlouiscathedral.org/convent-museum.

Signs and Wonders

Before Our Lady of Prompt Succor was working miracles in New Orleans, she was busy in France. In the mid-1780s, Sister Ste. Félicité and two other Ursuline sisters at the Pont-Sainte-Esprit convent responded to a missionary call to work with the Ursulines in New Orleans. But political unrest prevented their departure.

Sister Ste. Félicité was in the convent attic one day and found a small plaster statue of the Blessed Mother and the Child Jesus. Her heart breaking at seeing the abandoned statue, she vowed, "My Good Mother, if you will quickly remove these obstacles, I shall carry this image of you to New Orleans, where I promise to do all in my power to have you honored."

The very next day, the story goes, the good news arrived that the King of Spain (Spain then controlled Louisiana) had granted the French sisters permission to travel to New Orleans. Sister Ste. Félicité kept her promise and brought the twelve-inch statue to America. On Good Friday 1788, Our Lady of Prompt Succor returned the favor: She spared the Ursuline Convent from the Great New Orleans Fire.

More miracles were waiting in the wings. During the French Revolution in 1792, Sister Ste. Michel Gensoul and other Ursuline sisters in Pont-Sainte-Esprit were forced to abandon their convent, conceal their identities, and live and dress as laywomen — or face the guillotine.

Some years later, Sister Ste. Michel — now living as Agathe Gensoul — and another "lay Ursuline" started a boarding school for girls in

Montpellier, France. One day, Agathe received a letter from her cousin, Mother Ste. André Madier, head of the Ursuline Convent in New Orleans, Louisiana. More sisters were needed there to tend to the sick and teach the girls. Agathe sought permission from her bishop to go. The bishop, fearing for the future of the Montpellier school, refused, saying, "The pope alone can give this authorization. The pope alone!"

The bishop was rather smug in his response. Everyone knew that Napoleon's army had taken Rome in 1808 and that communications with Pope Pius VII were disrupted. (In July 1809, the pope was kidnapped by Napoleon's minions and held prisoner for nearly five years.) Nevertheless, Agathe wrote a letter to the pope requesting his permission. According to lore, the letter lay in her desk for several months. One day she was inspired to pray, "O most Holy Virgin Mary, if you obtain a prompt and favorable answer to my letter, I promise to have you honored in New Orleans under the title of Notre Dame de Prompt Secours" ("Our Lady of Prompt Succor").

"The next day the letter was on its way to Rome," reported Br. Gerald Muller, CSC, in *Our Lady Comes to New Orleans.* "It was March 19, 1809 — Saint Joseph's feast day." The pontiff's answer was dated April 28, 1809! The pope's reply was a double miracle: It was both quick and favorable!

Agathe commissioned a life-size wooden statue of Our Lady of Prompt Succor, painted in gold. Our Lady's swirling robes appear to be moving, as though she's in a rush to answer a prayer. She holds in her arms the Child Jesus, partially covered with a fold of her gold mantle.

In 1810, Agathe — now Mother Ste. Michel — and her Ursuline charges sailed for America. Traveling with them was Our Lady of Prompt Succor. It was at her feet that the Ursuline sisters and citizenry prayed before the Battle of New Orleans: "Our Lady, hasten to help us!"

The New World hasn't been the same since.

Our Lady of Prompt Succor

The people of New Orleans love their Lady! When Archbishop Francis Janssens asked the women of the Archdiocese of New Orleans to donate their gold and jewels to make crowns for Our Lady of Prompt Succor and Child, they gave enough jewels — amethysts, emeralds, opals, rubies, sapphires, topaz, and turquoise — to make two sets of crowns each for Our Lady of Prompt Succor and the Sweetheart statues. One set of crowns is adorned with precious stones, the other set with semiprecious gems.

On November 10, 1895, by decree of Pope Leo XIII, Archbishop Janssens canonically crowned the statue, gilded in gold, the first statue so crowned in the United States (see St. Augustine, Florida, site 12.) Our Lady's spectacular crown features a jeweled star at the top; the Child's crown, a cross of red rubies.

Our Lady's feast is January 8, the date of her victory over the British in 1815.

PIERRE PART

In 1882, high flood waters invaded the Catholic church in Pierre Part, a small town in the bayous of eastern Louisiana. When the waters receded, the Acadians noticed something amazing: A small statue of the Virgin Mary had fallen off her perch and landed in the water — on her feet! Other statues had deteriorated in the flood waters, but not Mary. Some thought it "a miracle," wrote Wildy L. Templet, a Pierre Part native, in *Pierre Part — Belle Riviere Down Home.*

Was someone looking out for Mary? The church was dedicated to Saint Joseph, her Helpmeet.

The little acrobat statue was placed in the church sacristy. In 1902, she was moved to a place of homage on a tiny island in a bay across from the church. Weekly, the priest and his flock would row their little boats to the little island and pray the Rosary. Seven years later, a larger Mary statue found its way to the island, and the little statue was buried nearby.

It wasn't Mary's only "voyage" on the bayous. In the 1930s, the chapel boat *Mary Star of the Sea*, pulled by the motorboat *St. Francis Xavier*, traversed the bayous, visiting outlying missions that were otherwise inaccessible. The priest in Pierre Part offered Mass, heard confessions, and baptized babies on the chapel boat. *Mary Star of the Sea* reeled in "the fish."

Parishioners didn't forget their Mother on **Virgin Island**, as the speck of land came to be called. A footbridge was built to the island and a marker placed. It reads, "Virgin Island commemorates the Blessed Virgin who the people of Pierre Part believe intervened to save lives in natural disasters from 1882–1976." A blue-robed Virgin stands in a gazebo-shrine, looking out for her husband's church across the bay.

Mass on Virgin Island is offered twice a year, on the second Saturday in May and October. You can come by foot, car, houseboat, or pirogue.

Come to Mary: 3304 Highway 70S, Pierre Part, LA 70339. (985) 252-6008. sjworker.org.

BAYOU GOULA
17

Bigger isn't necessarily holier in Mother Mary's eyes. When you step inside the tiny **Madonna Chapel** at Bayou Goula, on the Great River Road in southern Louisiana, a mighty peace begins to flow. And no wonder — it's a chapel of miracles.

As the story goes, Antonio Gullo's oldest son fell seriously ill. Gullo, a Sicilian immigrant and sugarcane farmer, invoked Our Lady's intercession and pledged to build her a chapel if the boy recovered. The boy's health returned, and in 1903 Gullo erected his tiny chapel of thanksgiving. The octagon-shaped chapel was so tiny that only a priest and an altar boy could fit inside; worshipers sat in a pew outside.

The Mississippi River levee changed over the years, and the chapel, built of Louisiana cypress and now topped with a quaint steeple, was moved to its present location facing the river. The chapel was squared off and "enlarged" to its approximate nine-foot-square shape.

Adorned with an Italian statue of the Madonna, the wee chapel became a "cathedral of the heart" for Italian and Sicilian immigrants. In gratitude for miracles and favors received, they gave Our Lady the most precious things they had: They pinned their wedding rings, bracelets, and Old World jewelry to her mantle and gown. She was their Queen and had to look the part.

The Madonna Chapel was anything but tiny in Victor Messina's life. As a young boy, he told Marion Amberg in a *St. Anthony Messenger* article on little chapels, he would go to the chapel and pour out

Crucifix and island — Virgin Island, Pierre Part, Louisiana

his tender heart to the Blessed Mother: "Mary, you know I want to be a priest when I grow up, and I'm asking you to open the way."

Our Lady opened the way and Father Messina was ordained a priest for the Diocese of Baton Rouge.

Dubbed the "smallest church in the world" by *Ripley's Believe It Or Not*, the picturesque white chapel with a miniature apse is just big enough for an altar, a kneeler, and several people — if everyone holds their breath. Little statues of Our Lady of Grace dot the chapel lawn, a white picket fence adding to the postcard scene.

Shortly after it was completed in 1903, the first Assumption Day Mass was held at the roadside chapel. The tradition continues today, with hundreds of worshipers gathering on the front lawn for

the special once-a-year Mass in honor of Mary, who was whisked body and soul into heaven. The annual celebration is also a miracle of its own, devotees claim. It always rains in Bayou Goula during August, but on this day the skies clear.

The chapel is kept locked to keep the animal "pilgrims" out. You can find the key in a box next to the door.

Come to Mary: 28527 LA-405, Plaquemine, LA 70764. (877) 310-8874. map.ibervilleparish.com /listing/madonna-chapel.

---

17. "The Smallest Church in the World" — Madonna Chapel, Bayou Goula (Plaquemine), Louisiana

MIDWEST

Grand Forks

Bismarck ★   Fargo

Duluth

28

Minneapolis

35

St

29

Rapid City   ★ Pierre

30   90

Sioux Falls

31

Sioux City

29

Des

90

Omaha

36   Lincoln ★

38

37   35

Kansas City   Sp

32

Topeka ★   St

Jefferson City

39

Wichita

44   Sp

Michigan

(18) MIO

Our Lady of the Woods Shrine in Mio (pronounced My-o) didn't begin with a miracle. The
miracle is who built it: Good folks from many walks
of life and religious denominations banded together
to create this monumental attraction honeycombed
with niches and grottoes. It began with a prayer and
a promise.

In 1945, one story goes, Fr. Hubert Rakowski
was shoveling knee-deep snow to clear a path for
his flock to attend Sunday Mass at St. Mary Catholic Church in Mio, a rural town in Michigan's Upper
Mitten (the shape of Michigan resembles a mitten).
The young Franciscan friar paused, looked up at the
humble frame church, and asked God to bless the
struggling mission and make it a prospering parish.
In return, he promised to build a special shrine in
honor of the Blessed Mother.

Heaven heard. The mission prospered and became a parish in 1951, with Father Rakowski as its first pastor.

Then something wonderful happened. In a real-life version of the folktale *Stone Soup*, local businesses, civic groups, and Protestant churches embraced Father Rakowski's vision for a shrine. A Lutheran widow in Ann Arbor, Michigan, donated a white Italian marble statue of Our Lady of Lourdes in memory of her husband. Two Baptist home builders erected a twenty-four-foot cross of tubular steel. Businesses provided materials, labor, and expertise.

In July 1953, with two borrowed shovels and nary a penny, Father Rakowski broke ground for the shrine. Resting on footings eight feet deep and four feet wide, the triangular-shaped mountain — erected of 25,000 tons of native Onaway limestone and an equal amount of cement — grew and grew until it was about 140 feet long and forty-three feet high. Much of the work was done by hand, with the aid of a huge scaffold, a homemade elevator, and wheelbarrows.

During the shrine's dedication weekend in September 1955, over 20,000 pilgrims and tourists descended upon the holy mountain. Some 33,000 medals of the shrine were given away; many of the medal wearers were non-Catholic. Before long, pilgrimage groups were descending upon the shrine. One group from Flint, Michigan, in 1964 was a sight to behold. Eighty nuns — in full habit — arrived in a fleet of brand-new Buick convertibles! Their outing had been sponsored by a Flint car dealership.

According to the shrine souvenir booklet, everything about this mountain is spiritually significant. The five steps ascending to the shrine represent the five decades of the Rosary; the waterfalls, the flow of God's blessings in our lives; and the bronze deer, Psalm 42:1, "As a deer longs for flowing streams, / so longs my soul for you, O God." The left and right wings of the shrine curve inward, as though Our Lady is embracing her visitors and the world at large.

The shrine's left wing shelters an altar and the Pietà Grotto, while the right wing — with three niches — celebrates Michigan's natural beauty and resources and is interwoven with Christian symbolism. The upper niche, with a bear statue and a cross (for Jesuit missionary Fr. Jacques Marquette), signifies the Upper Peninsula. The Straits of Mackinac and the Holy Trinity are represented in the middle alcove. The lower niche denotes the Lower Peninsula and sports a statue of Saint Hubert, patron of hunters, a stag at his side — proof that God is in the hunting, pilgrim-hunters quip.

The popular tourist attraction also imitates life: You can't see the shrines for the Shrine. Tourists

must "travel" to each individual shrine to appreciate the Carrara marble statuary and glean its spiritual meaning. Shrines honoring Mary's earthly visits are Our Lady of Fátima, Portugal (1917); Our Lady of Guadalupe, Mexico (1531); Our Lady of La Salette, France (1846); and Our Lady of Mount Carmel, England (1251). The near life-size statue of Our Lady of Lourdes, France (1858), stands near the top of "Mount Mio," a kneeling Bernadette statue below.

Nestled in the backside of the mountain is the Holy Family Grotto; its tunnel-like passageway reminiscent of the catacombs of Rome. Another cave houses a spectacular life-size mosaic of the wonder-working image of Our Lady of Czestochowa, minutely detailed even down to the scars on the Virgin's face. Outside, high up on the mountain, is the Assumption of Mary statue.

Greeting visitors near the shrine entrance is a figure of Christ the King. Other prayer stops include a statue of St. Francis of Assisi, the Stations of the Cross, and a large Calvary scene.

Our Lady of the Woods Shrine is always open, the mountainous retreat changing colors with the light and the seasons. It's particularly dramatic in the winter, when newly fallen snow glistens like diamonds from heaven. An annual outdoor Mass with a Rosary is celebrated on August 15, feast of the Assumption of the Blessed Virgin Mary.

Come to Mary: 100 Deyarmond Street, Mio, MI 48647. (989) 826-5509. olwshrine.org.

Our Lady of the Woods Shrine, Mio, Michigan

Signs and Wonders

When you feel compelled to say a prayer, say it: God might be at work! That's the testimony of one pilgrim who visited Our Lady of the Woods Shrine on July 28, 2019.

"I was in awe and couldn't see more [of the shrine] fast enough," said the pilgrim in the shrine's newsletter *Rejoicing in Faith*. When she reached the Pietà Grotto, she felt urged to light a candle and say a prayer for Renee, who had just been diagnosed with lung cancer. "I then walked out and around the back of the shrine and felt a strange tingling throughout my entire body."

Nine days later, on August 5, the pilgrim received word that Renee was fine. Doctors said the cancer was gone!

• • • • •

A fourteen-foot-long wooden rosary tells another story. Many years ago, the rosary was stolen from the Holy Family Grotto. How does such an enormous rosary — nearly a story-and-a-half tall — go missing? You can't exactly carry it in your pocket.

Decades passed. One day, in 2007, there came a knock at the rectory door. A young man was standing there with the giant rosary in his arms. "My mother stole this from the shrine a long time ago," he said. "She is now on her deathbed and wanted to return it before she dies." The rosary was intact, with no evidence of damage.

There's power in the rosary — even a stolen one!

• • • • •

Many years ago, two magnolia trees were donated to the shrine. Magnolia trees generally do not thrive in northern climes as cold as Mio's. Yet these two trees not only prospered, but come spring their blooms cast a fragrant aroma over the shrine grounds.

In 2012, Fr. Santiago M. Hoyumpa, pastor of St. Mary Catholic Church and Our Lady of the Woods Shrine, decided to reinstate the outdoor Mass on August 15, feast of the Assumption of the Blessed Virgin Mary. For many years, the annual Mass had been a pilgrimage tradition attended by tourists and locals alike.

That year the two magnolia trees didn't bloom in the spring as usual — they waited until mid-August! Like flowers from heaven, the trees provided blooms for the outdoor Mass. Shortly after Mary's feast, the flowers fell off the trees.

Ohio

19 ▶ NORTH JACKSON

Never say never to the Blessed Mother — she has a way of making things happen! That's the phenomenal story of the **Basilica and National Shrine of Our Lady of Lebanon** at North Jackson.

One day in 1960, Msgr. Peter Eid, a Maronite priest, was driving in rural northeast Ohio when he noticed a sign: Property for Sale, 80 Acres. His eyes lit up at the long frontage, the evergreens of a state forest, and the nearby turnpike and lodging. "That's it!" he thought. "A perfect spot for a shrine to Our Lady."

According to shrine history, the priest contacted the seller, a Protestant, and was roundly rejected. "I will never sell to a Catholic," she adamantly declared.

"But a House of Prayer would be a much better use of the property than a junkyard or a supermar-

Replica of shrine tower in Harissa, Lebanon — Basilica and National Shrine of Our Lady of Lebanon, North Jackson, Ohio

ket," Monsignor Eid pleaded. After three visits, Monsignor Eid told the woman, "This is my last visit, but I am going to call my friends and we will pray for nine days that God will tell you to sell us the land for a sanctuary for his Mother, Mary." He then asked his brother, Fr. Maroun Eid, and Fr. Maroun Abi Nader and his brother, Fr. Elias Abi Nader, to pray a novena for this very intention.

Before the nine days were up, the woman called Monsignor Eid and said, "Priest, come and take the land. Your Lady is bothering me in my sleep!" It's said that Our Lady told the woman in a dream that she wanted the property for a church. Never say never to Mary!

Construction began in 1964 on the shrine, a smaller replica of the Shrine of Our Lady of Lebanon at Harissa, Lebanon. The first American Maronite shrine of its kind, the 3,700-ton monument was built of stone like the original. Sixty-four steps spiral up the exterior of the fifty-foot, cone-shaped tower — one step for each Rosary prayer. Greeting you with open arms at the summit is the twelve-foot statue of Our Lady of Lebanon, carved of pink granite.

Nestled inside the base of the tower, like a mother enfolding her child, is the tiny Tower Chapel which seats thirty-five. Also on the shrine grounds are the Martyrs Meditation Trail, the Rosary and Saint Joseph Gardens, and the Basilica of Christ, the Prince of Peace, the second Maronite basilica in the world.

The popular Assumption pilgrimage, with candlelight processions, is held August 13–15.

Come to Mary: 2759 North Lipkey Road, North Jackson, OH 44451. (330) 538-3351. ourladyoflebanonshrine.com.

Signs and Wonders

On July 20, 1965, when the Virgin Mary statue was being set in place atop her tower at the Basilica and Shrine of Our Lady of Lebanon in North Jackson, a large cloud overhead suddenly turned "brilliant shades of pink, blue, and other colors of the rainbow," noted the basilica website. Onlookers interpreted the rainbow as a sign that Our Lady was smiling down on the shrine and her Maronite children.

In 2015, during the fiftieth anniversary celebration of the shrine, rain was falling on the faithful gathered for the outdoor Maronite liturgy. Suddenly, a rainbow appeared in the firmaments. Worshippers began snapping photos of the heavenly sign — a divine moment they didn't want to forget. "It's a miracle!" they said. "Mary is here with us!"

Two rainbows fifty years apart. What are the chances? Heaven's chances!

Our Lady of Lebanon

Perched on a hill overlooking the Mediterranean Sea at Harissa, Lebanon, Our Lady of Lebanon Shrine is a beacon of light to Christians and Muslims alike. While Muslims do not believe that Jesus is the Son of God, a chapter in the Quran is devoted to Maryam, an Arabic name for Mary. And doesn't Mary lead all her children — regardless of belief — to her son?

Dedicated in 1908, the bronze statue of Our Lady of Lebanon — twenty-eight-feet tall and weighing fifteen tons — was crafted in Lyons, France, and painted a gleaming white. The crowned Virgin stands with welcoming arms atop a conical tower of stone, over 100 steps spiraling to the top. Many pilgrims leave their shoes at the foot of the tower and make their way up barefoot, both as penance and a sign of reverence. Pilgrims can also pray in a chapel built into the tower base.

Our Lady of Lebanon's feast is celebrated on the first Sunday in May.

CAREY

20

When Our Lady wants to settle down in a place, she has a way of letting people know. How she came to dwell at the **Basilica and National Shrine of Our Lady of Consolation** in Carey is legendary. "Mary chose Carey," pilgrims say. Why else would this small town in north-central Ohio — an unlikely pilgrimage destination — become such a powerful miracle magnet?

But if Mary chose Carey, Fr. Joseph P. Gloden first chose Mary. While yet a seminarian, the Luxembourg native promised Mary to dedicate the first church he built or helped to build to Our Lady of Consolation. Around 1871, he was named pastor of Saint Nicholas Church in Frenchtown, Ohio.

Meanwhile, in nearby Carey, a small frame chapel was going up, its cornerstone dedicated to Saint Edward in 1867. In 1873, Father Gloden also took over the floundering Carey mission. He found thirteen families and a still-unfinished church.

"They were just as discouraged as they were few," wrote Father Gloden, his journal entries excerpted in a shrine booklet.

The priest helped finish the mission chapel and one day announced, "We are not yet at the end of our difficulties and we need a good, loving and powerful comforter." And so the church was rededicated to Our Lady of Consolation (Mary, Consoler of the Afflicted), satisfying Father Gloden's vow to Mary. He also commissioned a replica of Our Lady's statue in Notre-Dame Cathédrale in Luxembourg. A Frenchtown parishioner traveling to Luxembourg brought the statue back with him.

When Frenchtown parishioners saw the nearly three-foot-tall beauty — carved of oak and dressed in fine robes — they asked Father Gloden if they could carry the Lady in procession from Frenchtown to her new home in Carey, a distance of seven miles. Our Lady's solemn entry into Carey was set for May 24, 1875, the feast of Mary Help of Christians.

On the evening of May 23, a violent thunderstorm swept over the countryside. The rain poured all night, and it was still pouring the morning of the procession. Nevertheless, parishioners hastened to the church at the appointed time, their umbrellas wide open.

Behold, as the statue was brought out of the church, the rain parted like the Red Sea. "The sun pierced the clouds and was shining on the whole line of the procession all the way to about a mile from Carey," continued Father Gloden, "while it was continually thundering and lightning on both sides of us." Not one drop of rain fell on Our Lady or anyone in the procession. The Protestants gawked in awe at the phenomenon, the men removing their hats in reverence as Our Lady passed by.

"When we came to within a mile from the village of Carey," Father Gloden noted, "the clouds from both sides clashed together right in front of the procession, and it seemed impossible for us to reach the church before the rain would pour down upon us." The procession had scarcely entered the church when the "Red Sea" rolled back in. A cloudburst opened like a dam.

The procession wasn't the only miracle that day: Our Lady went right to work to console the afflicted. Leo, a Belgian farmer, fell to his knees before

Statue of Our Lady of Consolation — Basilica and National Shrine of Our Lady of Consolation, Carey, Ohio

the passing statue, prayers on his lips. His youngest child, Eugenie, was gravely ill and unable to retain food. When Leo returned home, he found the girl at the table eating her first food in four weeks.

Pilgrims began flocking to Mary in Carey. In 1900, it was decided to move the old church a short distance away and build a larger church to Our Lady on the old site. Romanesque in design, the new brick shrine, with upper and lower churches, was dedicated in 1925. The Conventual Franciscans arrived at the parish in 1912 and still minister there today.

On May 19, 1927, Our Lady vanished. Kidnapped! A ransom note, pinned to the rectory door, demanded $200 for her return. The thief telephoned Fr. Aloys Fish, OFM Conv, and stated his terms. He would send a messenger to collect the ransom and would divulge the statue's whereabouts if Father Fish promised not to follow the messenger. The priest agreed, and found the statue hidden in a public restroom behind the old church.

Our Lady was about to catch a serial thief. As the kidnapper was making arrangements with a messenger to fetch the ransom money, he was overheard by the sheriff's son, who notified his father. During the trial, the thief confessed to robbing no fewer than 7,000 churches over a twenty-year period! He even pried the offering boxes off the walls of Carey's shrine.

Pilgrims came by foot, train, and horseless carriage to Carey. During the Great Depression in 1937, over 50,000 pilgrims attended the August 15 procession and outdoor Mass in honor of Mary's Assumption. At least 18,000 confessions were heard that day alone.

To accommodate the popular processions, the shrine acquired thirty additional acres for the Shrine Park. Hundreds of trees were planted and an outdoor altar installed under a forty-five-foot-tall dome. Standing atop the dome is a twelve-foot, two-ton, gold-leafed bronze statue of Our Lady of Consolation (just try stealing this statue!). The Assumption Eve candlelight processions culminate here.

Though small in statue, Our Lady lives large in people's hearts. Hundreds of child-size dresses fill display cases in the lower church. The dresses, with matching outfits for the Christ Child, are handmade — each stitch, each adornment a petition or a prayer of thanksgiving. Of special note are Mary's original 1875 gown and her 1975 centennial dress, donated by the Hungarian people and decorated with Hungarian rhinestones.

Come to Mary: 315 Clay Street, Carey, OH 43316. (419) 396-7107. olcshrine.com.

Signs and Wonders

So many healings and miracles happen at the Basilica and Shrine of Our Lady of Consolation in Carey that the shrine features a "Miracle Monday" segment on Facebook. The following stories are reprinted, with permission, from Miracle Monday and edited for space.

• • • • •

On August 15, 1977, I made a pilgrimage to the shrine. The day was almost over and it was time to start for home. I was sitting in the church feeling very happy and also a little sorrow. The Mariachi violins were playing as Mexican pilgrims sang their traditional farewell to Mary.

I looked at Our Lady's statue and wondered if we had made her happy that day. For an instant, the face of her image became a blur. When I looked again, the face had taken on the qualities of a living person. She was smiling, very sweetly. It was over in a moment. I always thought this was a favor granted to me. But maybe other people would like to know that Our Lady smiles on us and is truly among us at the shrine in Carey.

• • • • •

My wife, Judy, was undergoing radiology treatments for breast cancer. She had been told that her radiologist was an atheist and a fallen away Catholic. But he was kind to Judy, and she liked him. Judy visited the shrine in Carey, and on her first trip back to the radiologist, he became visibly upset and started slamming things around.

"What's wrong?" Judy asked.

"Something's wrong with this equipment," he replied. "It shows that your tumor has shrunk and that's impossible."

Judy told him about our trip to Our Lady of Consolation Shrine.

"Bah!" he responded.

Even if the radiologist didn't believe it, he had just witnessed a miracle!

• • • • •

Before Bishop John Stowe, OFM Conv, was named shepherd of the Diocese of Lexington, Kentucky, he served as rector and pastor at the Carey basilica from 2010 to 2015. One day, the priest noticed a large woman running up and down the shrine steps. He thought surely she needed medical attention of some sort. He later learned that she had come in a wheelchair and was running up and down the steps in joy!

• • • • •

A young couple was having trouble conceiving a child and came to the shrine to pray. They met with Br. Jeffrey Hines, OFM Conv, during the annual August Novena and told him their story. The next year they came back to the shrine and looked up Brother Jeffrey. They had with them a large stroller — and their infant triplets!

Our Lady of Consolation

Devotion to Mary, Consoler of the Afflicted dates from the second century, but it wasn't until the bubonic plague struck Luxembourg that Our Lady "seized" the Grand Duchy. The cult here began on December 8, 1624 — the feast of the Immaculate Conception — when students at a Jesuit school and Fr. Jacques Brocquart, SJ, carried a Madonna statue to a spot outside Luxembourg City and placed it under a wooden cross. The following year a pilgrimage church was begun on this site.

In 1626, nearly the whole of Luxembourg fell ill with the bubonic plague. It's said the Grim Reaper took so many lives there weren't enough grave diggers or cemeteries to bury the dead. Nearly dead himself, Father Brocquart offered Mary a deal: If he lived, he would finish the chapel and dedicate it to Mary, Consoler of the Afflicted. The Glacis Chapel was dedicated in 1628 and the wooden Madonna enshrined inside.

A few decades later, both Luxembourg City and the Duchy of Luxembourg named Our Lady as their protectress. In 1794, the Madonna was moved to Notre-Dame Cathédrale in Luxembourg City, where her queenly vault runneth over with ex-votos. When the Grand Duchess Charlotte returned to Luxembourg after World War II, she gave Our Lady the rosary she had prayed with while in exile.

Our Lady of Consolation is portrayed holding the Christ Child in her left arm and a scepter in her right hand. Suspended from her right arm are a large silver heart and a large key. The key — with M-shaped teeth — represents Our Lady's ready access to the treasury of heavenly graces. Both Mother and Child wear crowns.

The Basilica and National Shrine of Our Lady of Consolation in Carey celebrates Our Lady's feast on May 25.

GARFIELD HEIGHTS

21

When Our Lady travels by sea, she's very picky about her ships. In 1939, an exact replica of the wonder-working image of Our Lady of Czestochowa was slated to leave Poland for the Marymount campus of the Sisters of Saint Joseph in Garfield Heights, a Cleveland suburb. The icon was painted by a Pauline Father and then blessed by the Pauline Fathers, custodians of Our Lady's shrine at Jasna Góra, Poland (see Doylestown, Pennsylvania, site 6). The Pauline Fathers also touched the replica painting to the original.

Perhaps that contact was what kept the replica out of troubled waters. The replica arrived at the dock five minutes too late and Our Lady missed her boat to Ohio. "That very ship, which left without the icon, was sunk on its way to America," noted a shrine pamphlet. "The next ship, carrying the icon, was the last one out of Poland before the ports were closed" due to the advent of World War II.

Measuring twelve by nineteen feet, the **Shrine of Our Lady of Czestochowa** was dedicated on October 1, 1939, one month after Nazi Germany invaded Poland on September 1. A rear sacristy adjoins the three-sided Byzantine-style brick shrine with altar, the attached pavilion protecting pilgrims from the elements.

On September 19, 1969, Cardinal Karol Wojtyla, the future Pope St. John Paul II, made an impromptu stop at the shrine during a visit to the United States. The Sisters of St. Joseph — founded in 1901 as the Polish Sisters of St. Joseph and known today as the Sisters of St. Joseph of the Third Order of St. Francis — joined the Polish cardinal in praying before the icon and singing hymns to the queen of Poland.

The shrine is now part of The Village at Marymount, a faith-based retirement community founded by the Sisters of St. Joseph.

Come to Mary: 12215 Granger Road, Garfield Heights, OH 44125. (216) 332-1100, (715) 341-8457. ssj-tosf.org.

The future Pope John Paul II visits the shrine in 1969 — Shrine of Our Lady of Czestochowa, Garfield Heights, Ohio

Indiana

22 ▶ SAINT MARY-OF-THE-WOODS

Can the promise of one woman end a world war? Maybe not, but the collective power of millions of prayers can work miracles.

In 1918 — like millions of souls across America and Europe — Mother Mary Cleophas Foley, general superior of the Sisters of Providence at Saint Mary-of-the-Woods, was begging heaven for the end of World War I. Upping her prayers one day, Mother Mary Cleophas pledged to build a grotto to Our Lady of Lourdes if the Great War ended that year before December 8, the feast of the Immaculate Conception.

Peace was declared on Armistice Day, November 11, 1918, and a mountainous grotto of stone was begun in a ravine on the motherhouse grounds, located near Terre Haute in western Indiana. According to an early shrine brochure, "Stones from Lourdes are embedded in the masonry, and the candlesticks used at the dedication Mass were those used at a Mass at Lourdes." The **Grotto of Our Lady of Lourdes** was dedicated on February 11, 1928, her feast day.

Replicating the famous shrine at Lourdes, France, Our Lady's statue graces an alcove near the top, a kneeling Bernadette statue prays below. Under Our Lady's feet is a cave with an altar; another cave houses a candle shrine. Growing on the craggy old stones are moss and ivy, making the century-old grotto appear even older.

Mother Mary Cleophas had upped her prayers and the Blessed Mother was about to up her presence in The Woods, as the motherhouse and college grounds are fondly called.

In 1925, Msgr. A. J. Rawlinson, chaplain of the Sisters of Providence, was traveling to Rome to promote the sainthood cause of Mother Theodore Guerin and stopped at Catholic University of America in Washington, D.C. There, he "chanced" to see an exquisite copy of Scipione Pulzone's painting *Mater Divinae Providentiae* (Our Lady of Divine Providence).

"How providential!" Monsignor Rawlinson surely thought. When Mother Theodore founded the Sisters of Providence at Saint Mary-of-the-Woods in 1840, and the girls' academy (now Saint Mary-of-the-Woods College) the following year, she placed both under the patronage of the Blessed Mother. The original painting of Our Lady of Providence just "happened" to be in Rome, his destination.

Monsignor Rawlinson visited the Church of San Carlo ai Catinari in Rome, where Pulzone's masterpiece had been revered for centuries. He then brought the devotion back to the sisters at The Woods, where she is venerated as Our Lady of Prov-

idence, Queen of the Home.

Located in the Church of the Immaculate Conception on the motherhouse grounds, the **National Shrine of Our Lady of Providence** will steal your heart. The replica painting of *Mater Divinae Providentiae*, by Italian artist Pompeo Coccia, is irresistible! The Child, with striking reddish-blonde hair, pays no heed to the viewer; his gaze is focused solely on his Mother. The shrine is known for answered prayer, especially in matters related to the family.

A true pioneer of faith, Saint Theodore's spirit inhabits Saint Mary-of-the-Woods. Her legendary life and devotion to Mary are immortalized in her namesake shrine, where her remains rest. "It is not admirable to see how much the Blessed Virgin loves us?" the saint once asked.

Come to Mary: 1 Sisters of Providence, Saint Mary-of-the-Woods, IN 47876. (812) 535-3131, (800) 860-1840. spsmw.org.

In addition to the Grotto, Saint Mary-of-the-Woods, Indiana, is home to the National Shrine of Our Lady of Providence.

Signs and Wonders

Before Sr. Ann Paula Pohlman, a Sister of Providence at Saint Mary-of-the-Woods, Indiana, was born, her Irish mother promised Our Lady of Providence to name the baby in her honor. Marie Louise (Sister Ann Paula's given name) was not only named for Mary, but she also loved the color blue, the traditional color associated with the Blessed Mother. As a teenager, Marie always chose blue clothes when she bought something new. One day, she learned the origin of her fondness for blue.

"My mother revealed that she had promised Mary that if I, her first born, was healthy she would call me Mary and would dress me in blue," recalled Sister Ann Paula in a story on the congregation's website. "Since it was during the Great Depression she was not always able to fulfill the latter promise."

The Pohlman family devotion to Our Lady continues today. When Sister Ann Paula's seven siblings were married, each received a framed picture of Our Lady of Providence. Many of their children also received this picture on their wedding day, giving them unique bragging rights of sorts. It's not every couple who can say, "Our Lady came to our wedding!"

Our Lady of Providence

According to tradition, the title Our Lady of Providence is attributed to Mary's intervention at the wedding feast at Cana. When the wine had run out, the Blessed Mother alerted Jesus, who told the servants to fill six large stone jars with water and then said, "Now draw some out, and take it to the steward of the feast" (Jn 2:8). It was Jesus' first recorded miracle. Mary's intercession at Cana also earned her the accolade Queen of the Home.

Around 1580, the Italian artist Scipione Pulzone composed his immortal painting *Mater Divinae Providentiae* (Mother of Divine Providence). The Barnabite Fathers took possession of the masterpiece about 1663 and later created a shrine to Our Lady of Providence in the Church of San Carlo ai Catinari in Rome. Grateful pilgrims left votive tablets, like many pages of a book, ascribing their extraordinary favors to Lady Providence.

The painting depicts the Blessed Mother, adorned with a sheer veil, cradling the Holy Child, his "halo" of reddish-blonde hair pulling viewers into the painting. The Child's left fingers clasp his Mother's left index finger, as though saying, "From my infinite storehouse, provide good things to all who implore thy aid."

Our Lady of Providence's feast day is November 19.

23 ST. JOHN

No dream is too big for Mother Mary! That's the miracle story of Carl Demma and his mega statue of **Our Lady of the New Millennium** at St. John, a town in northwestern Indiana.

In 1941, Carl, a nine-year-old altar boy and a student at All Saints Catholic School on the South Side of Chicago, Illinois, got permission to skip classes in order to ride with two priests to a downtown Chicago bank. While the priests went inside to deposit the Sunday collection money, the lad waited in the car so they wouldn't get a parking ticket, reported Gail Jardine in *Our Lady of the New Millennium*. It was a hot day, and Carl got out of the hot car to cool off.

Glancing up at the skyline, Carl saw a breathtaking statue of the Virgin Mary standing atop a skyscraper. He was transfixed! When the priests returned to the car, they asked what he was gawking at. "The Blessed Mother," he told them, "she's watching over Chicago!"

The priests chuckled. The statue — the pinnacle of the Chicago Board of Trade Building — wasn't Mother Mary at all, but Ceres, the Roman goddess of agriculture. Terribly disillusioned, young Carl vowed to one day erect a statue of Mary so big that all of Chicago could see her.

Many people forget their childhood dreams, but not Carl Demma. Four decades later, in 1983, Demma, who now owned a couple of liquor stores but didn't imbibe himself, saw the embodiment of his boyhood vow. The thirty-two-foot stainless steel statue of the Immaculate Heart of Mary stopped in

Our Lady of the New Millennium stands tall at the Shrine of Christ's Passion, St. John, Indiana.

Chicago while being transported from the East Coast to her new home in Santa Clara, California (see site 50). Enamored with Our Lady's beauty, Demma later commissioned its sculptor, Charles C. Parks, to create another but different Lady statue. The projected cost: $500,000.

Not everyone was smitten with Demma's monumental dream. As the story goes, when Demma asked Cardinal Joseph Bernardin of the Chicago archdiocese for his support, the prelate replied, "Do you know how many hungry people I could feed with that money?" Demma, a daily Mass-goer, re-

butted in kind, "Remember John 12:8, when Jesus said the poor you'll always have with you."

Other clergy scoffed at Demma and dismissed him as a lunatic.

(The Archdiocese of Chicago would later embrace the statue. Cardinal Francis George, OMI, suggested the name Our Lady of the New Millennium to mark the Great Jubilee Year 2000 — from December 24, 1999 to January 6, 2001 — which included the first six days of the third millennium.)

Even life itself seemed to rail against Demma and his wife, Francine. In 1986, a couple of years into the project, their twenty-four-year-old daughter, Judi, died of a genetic blood disorder — the same disorder that had claimed the life of her eight-year-old sister Carla twenty years earlier. Then Demma's own health began to fail.

But Demma, like Mary herself, had given his fiat. There was no turning back, even when he had to sell one of his liquor stores to finance the statue himself.

Then, as though Mary was giving Demma a big thumbs-up, the couple was invited to a private Mass in Rome with Pope St. John Paul II. After the Mass, Demma gave the Pontiff a brochure of the giant Madonna and asked if he would bless the statue. The pope said yes — if Demma could get the statue to Saint Peter's Square!

Instead, heaven brought the pope and the nearly completed statue to St. Louis, Missouri. On January 26, 1999, during his pontifical visit to America, Pope John Paul II cruised by Mega Mary in his bulletproof popemobile and made the sign of the cross over her. Demma was transfixed again.

The statue was returned to the sculptor's studio in Delaware for finishing touches. On May 3, the

8,400-pound, nearly four-stories-tall Virgin arrived in Chicago. Throngs of spectators descended upon the statue, awestruck at her sheer size and mystical refulgence. She looked like a vision! The sun danced off her long tresses and peeked through the slits of her gown, made of welded stainless-steel ribbons. Her gentle face with big, round eyes and her heart-shaped hands, not quite closed in prayer, impart a mother's care. Pilgrims couldn't kiss her on the cheek, so they kissed their fingers and touched her gigantic toes instead.

One little boy exclaimed with wonder, "If Mary is this big, imagine how big Jesus is!"

Demma died in 2000, at age sixty-eight, a year after the statue was completed. His boyhood vow had come to pass: Our Lady of the New Millennium was so big that all of Chicago really could see her!

Francine Demma stepped into her husband's shoes and for the next decade scheduled Our Lady's appearances. Millennium Mary — mounted on a Marian-blue flatbed truck equipped with a hydraulic lift to raise and lower her — was driven to dozens of churches and ethnic festivals around the region. Everywhere Mary went, onlookers stopped to gaze and pray.

Her traveling days over, Our Lady is now permanently enthroned at the Shrine of Christ's Passion in St. John, Indiana, where her mega-presence inspires pilgrims to live large for Mama Mary and Jesus, Our Lord.

Come to Mary: 10630 Wicker Avenue (US Highway 41), St. John, IN 46373. (855) 277-7474, (219) 365-6010. shrineofchristspassion.org.

Signs and Wonders

Wherever Our Lady of the Millennium went, miracles followed. A disabled man prayed at her feet and regained his power to walk. One inebriated man, driving by the illuminated statue at night, hit the brakes, fell to his knees, and bellowed, "I repent! I repent!" In Lemont, Illinois, noted Gail Jardine in *Our Lady of the New Millennium*, spectators reported seeing a flock of birds in flight break formation and form a living crown over Mary's head.

Couples got engaged in her presence. Families long estranged were reconciled at her feet. Mega Mary "grew" the faith of many: Atheists were converted, and many lapsed Catholics returned to the Church. She even commanded the respect of gangs. When the statue appeared in high-crime areas of Chicago, neighborhood gangs patrolled the streets, keeping Our Lady and her pilgrims safe.

Our Lady of the New Millennium

Our Lady's personal data never fails to impress.

Height: Thirty-three feet, eight inches. Because of a miscalculation, she stands one foot, eight inches taller than sculptor Charles C. Parks' first mega-Madonna in Santa Clara, California.

Weight: 8,400 pounds, or nearly twenty-one pounds per inch of height.

Even more impressive is the bulldog faith

that built it.

When Carl Demma commissioned Parks to build Millennium Mary about 1984, he couldn't have imagined the hurdles ahead of him. Everyone doubted him, even the Archdiocese of Chicago. His health problems mounting, he would tell his doctor, "Keep me going so I can finish the statue."

Demma wasn't enamored with Mary only because she was the Mother of God; Mary also represented the women in his life. "She is my mother; she's my aunt; she's my cousin; she's my friend," he once said. "In every woman ... there's a little bit of Mary."

But where would the $500,000 come from to complete the statue? The colossal artwork had been in the "works" for ten years. Demma would find some money, and the sculptor would work until the money gave out. One day, Demma remembered his Italian grandmother telling him, "If you appeal to Saint Anthony (the patron of lost and found) on his feast day, he won't turn you down." So Demma and his wife, Francine, traveled to Padua, Italy, to visit the Basilica di Sant'Antonio di Padova on June 13, the saint's feast day.

The church was jammed with pilgrims petitioning the wonderworker. But Saint Anthony hadn't heard anything yet. Demma began yelling at the saint like a wild man, recounted Gail Jardine in *Our Lady of the Millennium*.

"I've never asked for favors; I've never asked for things in my life," he shouted, "but I really need a favor this time. Let me do it. I know I can do it. I can help the people of Chicago!"

A clergyman asked Demma who he was talking

to. Nobody talked to Saint Anthony that way.

"He has to hear my voice!" Demma replied.

At that very moment, Demma got his answer, continued Jardine. "Saint Anthony told me in so many words, 'Okay, big shot, put your money where your mouth is. Sell your business. Build the statue.'"

And so Demma sold a liquor store — his retirement cushion.

Fifteen years after Demma had commissioned Our Lady's statue — and fifty-eight years after he first envisioned a statue of Mary big enough for all of Chicago to see — Our Lady of the New Millennium arrived in the Windy City. There is no greater love than a boy for his Mother, Mary.

ST. MEINRAD

Monte Cassino Shrine has nothing to do with casinos or gambling — Monte Cassino is the hilltop abbey in Italy where St. Benedict of Nursia lived in the sixth century — but Our Lady of Monte Cassino is a sure bet for halting a deadly epidemic. That's the testimony of this Old World-style shrine, erected by Benedictine monks of Saint Meinrad Archabbey in 1870.

In December 1871, smallpox broke out in the village of St. Meinrad, in southern Indiana, and took the lives of several children and two adults. During the Christmas holiday, "four persons of the monastery were ill with the disease," wrote Alfred Kleber, OSB, in *History of St. Meinrad Archabbey 1854–1954*. "Since the students seemed to be specially [sic] susceptible to it, the worst was feared."

The fear was real: Smallpox killed thirty percent of its victims.

The monks and the students decided to make a novena to Our Lady of Monte Cassino. On January 5, 1872, every student who could walk made the pilgrimage to Monte Cassino Shrine, a hilltop stone chapel, where a Solemn Votive High Mass was offered. The pilgrimage was repeated on January 13, the final day of the novena.

Once the novena had begun, not one new case of smallpox broke out! In gratitude for the Virgin's help, Saint Meinrad students to this day make a yearly pilgrimage to the shrine on or near January 13.

As devotion to Our Lady of Monte Cassino grew, many marvelous cures were reported at the chapel. In 1886, noted a 125th anniversary booklet, parents brought their five-year-old disabled boy to Mary and prayed. The boy, who couldn't walk to the

shrine because of a hip disease, walked part of the way home. When a fleck of straw struck a girl's eye and caused loss of vision, she went to "see Mary"; her sight was restored. Another girl, born with a protruding intestine, was healed after being carried in prayer to Monte Cassino Shrine.

How could it be otherwise? The jewel-box chapel, decorated with cobalt-blue stained glass and paintings of Mary with cobalt-blue backdrops, is simply magnificent. Penned by an abbey monk, continued Kleber, this apt verse was chiseled in 1932 on a stone post:

Here, with Mother, rest a span;
Then go thy way a better man.

Pilgrims rest a span and then go their way … better in body, mind, and spirit.

Come to Mary: 13312 Monte Cassino Shrine Road, St. Meinrad, IN 47577. (800) 581-6905, (812) 357-6611. saintmeinrad.org/the-monastery /monte-cassino-shrine.

Monte Cassino Shrine, St. Meinrad, Indiana

LEOPOLD

The statue of **Our Lady of Consolation at St. Augustine Church** in Leopold tells a fascinating tale of mystery and intrigue. According to church history, three parish men, fighting for the Union army during the Civil War, were captured by Confederate forces and incarcerated at the notorious prisoner-of-war camp at Andersonville, Georgia.

The Andersonville Prison — a twenty-six-acre "cattle pen" crammed with 32,000 men — was a hellhole on earth. Prisoners were provided no shelter, scant food, and tainted water. If inmates didn't succumb from starvation or dysentery, they were attacked by mad dogs or fellow crazed prisoners. Nearly 13,000 of the 45,000 men corralled here died; that's roughly one death every hour for the fourteen months the prison was open. It's a wonder that anyone survived.

Staring death in the face, three Leopold soldiers of Belgian descent — Lambert Rogier, Henry Devillez, and Isadore Naviaux — turned to Our Lady of Consolation and made her a deal. If they made it out alive, one of them would travel to Belgium and have a replica made of Our Lady's statue that Devillez remembered seeing as a lad in an ancestral church. Miraculously, all three soldiers survived eleven months in the dastardly camp.

True to their covenant, Rogier sailed for Belgium and returned in 1867 with components of a statue: a head, two arms, and a stone slab for Our Lady's body, and a baby Jesus figure, reported Patricia Happel Cornwell in *The Criterion*, a publication of

the Archdiocese of Indianapolis.

The comely statue, about four feet tall, was assembled, dressed in fine robes, and enshrined on Mary's side altar. In traditional iconography (see Carey, Ohio, site 20), Our Lady holds a scepter in her right hand, a silver heart and a key hanging from her right arm. In her left arm is the Child Jesus, holding an orb with a cross on top. Both Mother and Child wear crowns and are dressed in colors according to the liturgical season.

But there's another "statuesque" story that circulates around these back roads of southern Indiana. Some contend that Rogier stole the statue, sparking an international incident. When King Leopold I of Belgium, who was reportedly furious about the statue's disappearance, learned the icon was in the village of Leopold — founded in 1842 and named in his honor — he was so flattered that he allowed the statue to stay at St. Augustine Church.

Another statue of Our Lady of Consolation graces a grotto on the church grounds. It's said that some devotees take Our Lady to their graves and have her image etched on their tombstones.

Come to Mary: 18020 Lafayette Street, Leopold, IN 47551. (812) 843-5143. archindy.org /parishes/listings/089.html, archindy.org /criterion/local/2018/06-29/archives.html.

CHAMPION

You're standing on miracle ground at the **National Shrine of Our Lady of Good Help** in Champion. In October 1859, the Blessed Mother appeared three times on this hallowed site to Adele Brise, a Belgian native. Twelve years later, in 1871, the Great Peshtigo Fire roared toward the apparition site and its wooden chapel, incinerating everything in its path. Incredibly, the firestorm stopped at the chapel fence line!

This supernatural chain of events would never have happened if Adele hadn't heeded the words of her confessor back in Belgium: "Obey your parents, and go to America."

Born January 30, 1831, to Lambert and Marie Catherine Brise at Dion-le-Val, Belgium, Marie Adele Joseph — like many visionaries to whom Our Lady has appeared — was poorly educated but pious of soul. She was also blinded in one eye due to an accident. At the time of her first Communion, Adele and several girlfriends promised the Blessed Mother to join a convent in Champion, Belgium, and devote their lives as foreign missionaries. The other girls heeded their promise, but Adele continued to live and work at home.

When her parents decided to immigrate to America, Adele felt conflicted: She had vowed to become a religious sister. Adele sought the advice of her confessor. "If God wills it, you will become a sister in America," he told her. "Go, I will pray for you."

In June 1855, Lambert, his wife, and their three daughters — Esperance, Adele, and Isabel — sailed for America and bought 240 acres near Robinsonville (now called Champion), near Green Bay in northeast Wisconsin. The pioneer family settled in and worked the land.

In early October 1859, Adele, twenty-eight years old, was walking to the grist mill with a sack of wheat on her head, when a lady in white appeared between two trees — a maple and a hemlock. Frightened, Adele froze like a statue. The lady slowly vanished, leaving behind a white cloud. When Adele returned home, she told her parents about the mysterious encounter. Perhaps it was a poor soul from purgatory in need of prayer, they reasoned.

The following Sunday, October 9, Adele, her sister Isabel, and a neighbor woman were walking to Mass at Bay Settlement, eleven miles distant, when they came upon the same two trees. "O there is that lady again," a startled Adele told them. Again, the lady disappeared in a white mist.

After Mass, Adele told Fr. William Verhoeff, OSC, about the "lady in the trees." The priest told Adele if the lady were a messenger from heaven, she would see her again and to ask in God's name who she was and what she wanted.

Adele and companions began the long trek home. As they neared the trees, Adele again saw the lady, clothed in a radiant white gown that fell to her feet, a yellow sash around her waist. Her golden wavy hair fell over her shoulders, a crown of stars surrounded her head. Adele dropped to her knees.

What happened next, in Adele's own words, was recorded by Sr. Pauline LaPlante, OSF, and published for posterity in Sister M. Dominica's booklet *The Chapel: Our Lady of Good Help.* Sister Pauline had heard the story many times from Adele's own lips:

> "In God's name, who are you, and what do you want of me?" asked Adele as she had been directed.
>
> "I am the Queen of Heaven who prays for the conversion of sinners, and I wish you to do the same. You received Holy Communion this morning and that is well. But you must do more. Make a general confession and offer Communion for the conversion of sinners. If they do not convert and do penance, my Son will be obliged to punish them."
>
> "Adele, who is it?" said one of the women. "O why can't we see her as you do?" said another weeping.
>
> "Kneel," said Adele, "the Lady says she is the Queen of Heaven." Our Blessed Lady turned, looked kindly at them, and said, 'Blessed are they that believe without seeing.'"
>
> "What are you doing here in idleness,"

continued Our Lady, "while your companions [her childhood friends who had entered religious life] are working in the vineyard of my Son?"

"What more can I do, dear Lady?" said Adele, weeping.

"Gather the children in this wild country and teach them what they should know for salvation."

"But how shall I teach them who know so little myself?" replied Adele.

"Teach them," replied her radiant visitor, "their catechism, how to sign themselves with the Sign of the Cross, and how to approach the sacraments; that is what I wish you to do. Go and fear nothing, I will help you."

The Queen of Heaven lifted her hands as if to beseech a blessing on Adele and companions and disappeared into the heavens.

For the next six years, Adele traveled by foot in "this wild country," sojourning up to fifty miles from home. Knocking on doors, she offered to do housework in exchange for the privilege of teaching the children the rudiments of the Faith. Nothing kept Adele from Our Lady's commission — not fatigue, not snow or heat, not even ridicule. Her childhood vow of laboring in "foreign missions" was coming to pass.

Meanwhile, Adele's father built a small log chapel, ten-by-twelve-feet, near the hallowed trees. Pil-

Stained glass image of Our Lady's apparition to Adele Brise —
National Shrine of Our Lady of Good Help, Champion, Wisconsin

GO AND FEAR NOTHING, I WILL HELP YOU

grims began flocking to the chapel and, two years later, a larger chapel went up. Over the exterior entrance appeared the French words, "*Notre Dame de Bon Secours, priez pour nous* (Our Lady of Good Help, pray for us)." On one wall hung eight crutches, left by healed cripples.

Around 1864, Adele and a small band of like-minded women formed a community of Secular Franciscans. While the women wore a religious habit and were called Sister, they took no vows and could leave whenever they wished. A wooden convent and a boarding school went up. Instead of Adele going to the children, they now came to her. The sisters taught subjects in French and English, with Sister Adele giving the religious instruction.

On October 8, 1871, calamity struck northeast Wisconsin. Known as the Great Peshtigo Fire, the firestorm — the deadliest fire in American history — roared like a tornado across both sides of the bay of Green Bay and devoured whole towns. On the east side of the bay, the wooden Chapel of Our Lady of Good Help stood directly in its fiery path.

Terror stricken, farm families drove their livestock to the chapel grounds. Sister Adele and the people processed outside the chapel, on their knees, with a statue of Mary and prayed the Rosary. When the wind and smoke began to suffocate them, they turned and went in another direction. Prayer was their only hope — tongues of fire were licking at the chapel fence! Through it all, Adele trusted in Our Lady's words, "I will help you."

In the early morning hours of October 9 — the twelfth anniversary of Our Lady's final apparition to Adele — heaven sent a downpour and squelched the fire. Our Lady of Good Help did help!

Everything for miles around was burned, except for the convent, school, chapel, and the five acres of land dedicated to the Virgin Mary, continues Sister Dominica's account. They "shone like an emerald isle in a sea of ashes."

If anyone doubted Sister Adele's visions of the Blessed Mother, they doubted no more. Pilgrims began coming to the chapel in droves. A larger chapel of brick was erected in 1880, and a new brick convent and school in 1885. A few years later, the village of Robinsonville changed its name to Champion, fulfilling, in a sense, Adele's girlhood promise to the Blessed Mother to enter the convent at Champion, Belgium.

Sr. Adele Brise died on July 5, 1896, at age sixty-six, and was buried in a small cemetery near the chapel. Six years later, the two remaining sisters joined the Franciscan Sisters at Bay Settlement (now the Sisters of St. Francis of the Holy Cross). The Bay Settlement sisters ran Adele's boarding school until it closed in 1929, and continued caring for the chapel property until 1992. The sisters are credited with preserving the holy site and its miraculous history.

In 1941, the present red-brick chapel of Tudor Gothic design went up. The altar in the Apparition Chapel, the upper level, stands over the apparition site. In the Apparition Oratory, the lower crypt, a statue of Mary graces the spot where she visited Adele between the two trees.

On December 8, 2010, the feast of the Immaculate Conception, Bishop David L. Ricken of the Diocese of Green Bay proclaimed Adele's apparitions to be authentic and true. The National Shrine of Our Lady of Good Help is the first and only Church-approved Marian apparition site in the United States.

Major pilgrimage events include the annual Walk to Mary (walktomary.com), held the first Saturday in May, and the October 8 candlelight Rosary procession that commemorates the shrine's miraculous save from the Great Peshtigo Fire in 1871.

The hallowed grounds also include Sister Adele's grave, the 1885 brick convent and schoolhouse where Sister Adele and her sisters once taught, and a tiny Belgian roadside chapel — one of dozens of roadside chapels that dot the surrounding countryside.

Come to Mary: 4047 Chapel Drive, Champion, WI 54229. (920) 315-0398. championshrine.org.

Signs and Wonders

On October 8, 1871, the Great Chicago Fire raced across the Windy City and produced a Marian miracle of its own (see Chicago, Illinois, site 27). That same night an even mightier blaze, the Great Peshtigo Fire — the deadliest inferno in American history — raged across northeast Wisconsin, a heavily forested area. Fueled in part by a prolonged drought, the firestorm consumed 2,400 square miles, roughly the size of the State of Delaware. Some 1,500 to 2,500 souls perished in the blaze. Many bodies were never found.

Racing ahead of the fireball, Fr. Peter Pernin, pastor of St. Mary's Church in Peshtigo, ran to the church and rescued the wooden tabernacle with the Blessed Sacrament. He loaded the tabernacle in a wagon and then pushed the wagon into the Peshtigo River. The priest then jumped into the river to save himself.

The entire town of Peshtigo burned to the ground, including Father Pernin's church.

Three days later, the tabernacle was found floating on a log, unharmed! According to Father Pernin in *The Great Peshtigo Fire: An Eyewitness Account*, the tabernacle, painted a snowy white, escaped without a trace of damage. No charring. No burned edges. When Father Pernin opened the tabernacle door, he found the Host and monstrance to be perfectly intact.

The Miraculous Tabernacle is displayed at the Peshtigo Fire Museum, where Father Pernin's church once stood, during the summer months, and at St. Mary's Church in Peshtigo the other months.

Peshtigo Fire Museum: 400 Oconto Avenue, Peshtigo, WI 54157, (715) 582-3244, peshtigofiremuseum.com; **St. Mary's Church:** 171 South Wood Avenue, Peshtigo, WI 54157, (715) 582-3876, stmaryjosephedwardparish.org.

Our Lady of Good Help

While little is known about the devotional origins of Our Lady of Good Help, she has been a good help to multitudes, especially in France and Belgium. As early as the eleventh century, boatmen on the Seine River in France would stop to pray at Our Lady's chapel in the town of Bonsecours

(Good Help), near Rouen, hanging model boats as ex-votos. The chapel evolved and is known today as the Basilique de Notre-Dame de Bonse-cours.

In Péruwelz, Belgium, the piety dates from medieval times, when a picture of Our Lady in an oak tree was venerated as Our Lady Between Two Woods. The tree died about 1603 and two Mary statues were carved from its wood. One statue remained in Péruwelz, under the title Notre-Dame de Bon-Secours. In 1636, Our Lady's devotion surged when the town escaped the Black Plague. The centuries-old statue is venerated today at the Basilique de Notre-Dame de Bon-Secours in Péruwelz, about fifty miles from Dion-le-Val, where visionary Adele Brise was born.

When Our Lady appeared to Adele at Champion, Wisconsin, between two trees, she said, "Go and fear nothing. I will help you." Our Lady of Good Help has been helping pilgrims here ever since.

Sister Adele Brise

Illinois

(27) **CHICAGO**

Can miracles strike twice? It happened at the **Church of the Holy Family** in Chicago! Then again, Our Lady of Perpetual Help isn't your ordinary intercessor. When she intervenes, all of heaven and earth move, often in very dramatic ways.

Founded in 1857, Holy Family Church, as it was originally called, was destined for greatness. When Fr. Arnold Damen, SJ, began erecting the spectacular brick structure — the city's second-oldest surviving church — in what was then the outskirts of Chicago (now the Near West Side), scoffers asked where his flock would come from. The Dutch immigrant was known to say, "I shall not go to the people, I shall draw the people to me."

Did the flocks ever come! Chicago grew by leaps and bounds, and by the 1890s, Holy Family Church was reportedly the country's largest English-speaking parish and boasted over 25,000 members. Who wouldn't want to attend this magnificent Victorian Gothic church, described as a "European cathedral on the Illinois prairie?" It's a paradise in wood.

The high altar — fifty-two feet of elaborate woodcarving, with thirteen wooden statues set in illuminated niches — could spirit any doubting soul to heaven. Up in the second balcony, a hand-carved orchestra of twenty-nine wooden angels play musical instruments: violin, clarinet, French horn, trumpet, flute, harp, tambourine, even a banjo. If that didn't sweep folks off their earthly feet, the twelve round clerestory windows — Chicago's oldest stained glass — did.

On October 8, 1871, disaster struck the Windy City. Fire! A severe drought had prevailed across the region that summer, and Chicago was dry as a tinderbox. Fueled by high winds, the Great Chicago Fire consumed three-and-one-half square miles, destroyed some 17,500 buildings, and left more than 100,000 residents homeless. An estimated 300 souls perished in the blaze. (See Champion, Wisconsin, site 26.)

As Providence had it, Father Damen was conducting a parish mission at St. Patrick Church in Brooklyn, New York, that fateful night, when he was handed an urgent telegram in the confession box. A fire had started in parishioners Catherine and Patrick O'Leary's barn on De Koven Street, a few blocks from Holy Family Church. The church, with its mostly wooden interior, was in grave danger.

(The tale that Mrs. O'Leary's cow, Daisy, kicked over a lamp in the family barn and started the fire is a myth. A Chicago journalist later confessed to making the whopper up. In 1997, Mrs. O'Leary was formally absolved: The Chicago City Council's Com-

mittee on Police and Fire declared that neither she — nor Daisy — started the conflagration. To this day, nobody really knows how the fire began.)

Kneeling before the church altar in Brooklyn, Father Damen prayed most of the night, imploring heaven to save his church and the wooden cottages of his immigrant flock. "With tears streaming down his cheeks, he made a vow that if his petition were answered he would, for all time, keep seven lights burning" before an image of Our Lady of Perpetual Help, reported *Holy Family Parish Chicago*.

The winds shifted. Incredibly, the church and every one of the congregants' cottages — even the O'Leary house — were spared. "Iron, brick and stone structures melted like snow before the flames, but the wooden dwellings were unscathed," continued *Holy Family Parish Chicago*. The church was one of the few public structures to survive the Great Fire.

St. Ignatius College, adjacent to Holy Family Church and the forerunner of Loyola University Chicago, was also saved that day. The brick building is now part of Saint Ignatius College Prep, a private Jesuit high school.

A century passed. Chicagoans migrated to the suburbs, church membership dwindled, and the Victorian Gothic masterpiece fell into disrepair. In 1987, the Jesuit Province of Chicago announced plans to raze the grand church and replace it with a smaller, more utilitarian worship center. Parishioners wouldn't hear of it. They formed the Holy Family Preservation Society, a nonprofit, and began raising funds to restore the Chicago landmark.

High altar at Christmas — Church of the Holy Family, Chicago, Illinois

In mid-1990, another edict fell. The Jesuit Province informed Fr. George A. Lane, SJ, then pastor of Holy Family Church, and the Holy Family Preservation Society that they needed to have $1 million in cash by December 31 for church restoration, or the historic structure would be obliterated.

As Christmas neared, the Holy Family Preservation Society was still short of its $1 million goal. Following in Father Damen's footsteps, Father Lane invoked Our Lady of Perpetual Help (see "Our Lady of Perpetual Help" in the entry for site 4) and then launched a blitzkrieg media effort and a prayer campaign to move heaven and earth. Beginning on December 26, parishioners began holding nightly prayer vigils, with seven lights and an icon of Our Lady, on the front steps of the church. Media the nation over — from CNN to the Associated Press to *The New York Times* — followed the high spiritual drama. Would Our Lady save Holy Family Church from the wrecking ball?

On January 1, 1991, the cash was counted. Our Lady delivered — $1,011,000! Seven lights still burn before Our Lady's image in her church shrine. You'll also find the Blessed Mother in a painted carving of the Holy Family's flight to Egypt on Saint Joseph's side altar. Perhaps in a nod to Chicago's deep Irish roots, Joseph wears a derby hat.

Come to Mary: 1080 West Roosevelt Road, Chicago, IL 60608. (312) 492-8442. holyfamilychicago .org.

Signs and Wonders

Many stories are told of Father Arnold Damen and the mystical world that seemed to envelop him, but none are as compelling as that of the two acolytes. As recounted in *Holy Family Parish Chicago*, one stormy night two lads rang the rectory doorbell, summoning Father Damen to the sick bed of a dying woman. The priest followed the boys to a ramshackle house, heard the lady's confession, and gave her the last rites.

As Father Damen was getting ready to leave, the old lady said, "Father, may I ask who called you to me. I have been very ill and I have wanted a priest, but I had no one to send."

"Have you no boys of your own?" the puzzled priest asked.

"I had two boys who were acolytes of the Holy Family Church, but they are dead."

The woman died before morning.

As the story runs, the two acolyte statues in the church sanctuary commemorate that holy night, when two boys came down from heaven to help their dying mother up to the Celestial City of God.

Our Lady of The Holy Family

Our Lady gave birth to the Christ Child, but her role as the Blessed Mother also meant caring for the Holy Family. There were meals to cook, garments to mend, water to fetch at the Nazareth well, and a Child to instruct in the Jewish faith. It's possible that Mary even cut Jesus' and Joseph's hair.

Like women today, the Blessed Mother had umpteen daily household chores. But no matter the to-do list, she always honored her fiat — her "yes" — at the Annunciation. "Behold, I am the handmaid of the Lord," Mary told the Angel Gabriel in Luke 1:38, "let it be to me according to your word."

Mary said "yes" when she gave birth to Baby Jesus in a barn. She said "yes" when the Holy Family fled their homeland for Egypt to escape Herod's Slaughter of the Innocents. She said "yes" when Joseph died and left her a young widow. She said "yes" as her Son climbed Crucifixion Hill with his cross.

The Blessed Mother is still saying "yes" today. Whenever we invoke her name, she takes our prayer petitions to God and appeals on our behalf. The vaults of heaven are filled with miracles — big and small — attributed to Our Lady's intercession. She is Our Mother, after all.

The feast of the Holy Family is celebrated during the Octave of Christmas.

COLD SPRING

Who is your help in times of plague? Maria Hilf! In 1876, swarms of Rocky Mountain locusts — or grasshoppers, as the settlers called them — descended upon the Cold Spring area, in west-central Minnesota. Traveling in massive clouds up to forty miles wide and 150 miles long, the "demons with wings" reportedly measured up to two inches in length, with eyes like the head of a shingle nail.

The hoppers devoured fields and gardens to the quick (except for the peas — they detested peas), chomped on wooden fork handles, and attacked the laundry strung outside to dry. One farmer hung his jacket on a fence post and found only buttons when he returned. "They ate everything but the mortgage," lamented one immigrant. The holiest of hoppers even attended Mass. Altar boys were kept busy shooing them off the altar and the priest.

The Cold Spring infestation, however, was but a

flyspeck in an even greater plague. Migrating from Colorado about 1873, the locusts ate their way across Wyoming, Nebraska, South Dakota, and then invaded southwestern Minnesota. By 1876, the plague had possessed nearly two-thirds of the state, with reports of fields covered with locusts two to three inches deep.

Laura Ingalls Wilder, then a young girl living in Walnut Grove, Minnesota, recounted the scourge in her children's book *On the Banks of Plum Creek*: "The cloud was hailing grasshoppers. The cloud *was* grasshoppers. Their bodies hid the sun and made darkness. Their thin, large wings gleamed and glittered. … You could hear the millions of jaws biting and chewing." Before long, her Pa's wheat field was gone.

Farmers did everything in their might to stop the flying demons. They lit smudge pots to keep the critters in flight. "Hopper dozers" — large sheets of metal smeared with tar — were dragged by horses over fields to trap the pests in the sticky black goo. Other farmers tried to catch the hoppers with large, hooped burlap bags. Bounties were also offered.

"One farmer collected eighteen bushels of grasshoppers (100,000 per bushel) from a ten-acre field," reported Fr. Robert J. Voigt in his booklet *The Story of Mary and the Grasshoppers.* "One lad, four years old, made enough money at three cents a bushel to buy himself $2 boots."

The warm spring of 1877 brought another round of fear: Millions upon millions of locust eggs were ready to hatch. In hopes of staying the pestilence and

Grasshopper tympanum — Assumption Chapel, Cold Spring, Minnesota sparing the state further economic damage, Governor John S. Pillsbury declared April 26 a statewide day of prayer and fasting. He stated, in part, "Let us humbly invoke for the efforts we make in our defense the guidance of that hand which alone is adequate to stay 'the pestilence that walketh in darkness and the destruction that wasteth at noonday.'"

Theaters, bars, and businesses were shuttered, and church doors flung open.

Within days, the *St. Paul Dispatch* began reporting wondrous stories of deliverance. In some areas, a two-day snowstorm began the night of April 26 and froze the fledging hoppers in their tracks. In other areas, little red parasites appeared and began feasting

on the locust eggs as though they were caviar.

Yet other areas, including Cold Spring, were still jumping with the pests. According to a diary kept by Fr. Leo Winter, OSB, area pastor, and excerpted in *Amid Hills of Granite, A Spring of Faith,* the 1877 growing season was dismal to say the least. "[Farmers] did not see a trace of the potatoes they planted, and what they saw today was eaten away tomorrow."

One Saturday while saying Mass in honor of Our Lady, the young priest had a heaven-sent idea: What if the German-speaking settlers vowed, out of pure love, to erect a chapel to *Maria Hilf* — Mary Help (also translated as Mary, Help!) — to avert the plague? Weather permitting, Saturday Masses in honor of the Mother of God would be offered there for fifteen years and a yearly Mass on August 15. Folks agreed, and construction of a sixteen-by-twenty-six-foot frame chapel began on July 16, 1877.

Miraculously, the hoppers started leaving! The grasshoppers "walked into Plum Creek and drowned," continued Ingalls Wilder, "and those behind kept on walking in and drowning until dead grasshoppers choked the creek and filled the water and live grasshoppers walked across on them." Four days later, the author claimed, the remaining hoppers arose in a cloud and took their leave.

By August 14, the hilltop chapel at Cold Spring was finished. The following day — the feast of the Assumption of the Blessed Virgin Mary — Father Winter, with episcopal permission, dedicated the chapel to Maria Hilf and offered the first Mass. Carved by local farmer Joseph Ambroziz, a life-size wooden statue of Mother and Child was enthroned inside. Mother Mary holds the Child in her right arm, a scepter in her left hand.

"Lastly, it must be reported, that as soon as the promise was made and building begun, the grasshoppers departed by and by," testified Father Winter in a notarized document witnessed by six parishioners. "Today [September 8, 1877] none are to be found. Mary our Mother did help!"

Mary not only helped, but she may have vanquished the insect. According to the Smithsonian National Museum of Natural History, the Rocky Mountain locust is now believed to be extinct.

The "*Kapelle* on a hill" soon became known as Marienberg ("Mary Hill"). For many years, pilgrims climbed the steep earthen steps on their knees, offering a Hail Mary at each step. Then, on June 28, 1894, a twister picked up the little chapel and slammed it into a grove of oak trees. Everything was destroyed, except for Our Lady's statue.

Marienberg stood vacant for nearly six decades. In 1951, the *Kapelle* was rebuilt of local granite and dedicated the following year as **Assumption Chapel**. The statue of Mother and Child was again enthroned inside. Above the entrance, a tympanum depicts in granite relief the faith story of the chapel: Mary stands on a cloud, two grasshoppers kneel at her feet. At the top are the Latin words *Assumpta est Maria* ("Mary is assumed" [into heaven]).

The Grasshopper Chapel, as it's called locally, is always open to pilgrims in need of Mary's help. Traditions include an annual novena of weekly Masses for bountiful crops and a Mass of Thanksgiving on August 15.

Come to Mary: 22912 Chapel Hill Road, Cold Spring, MN 56320. (320) 204-1111. christcatholic.com/assumption-chapel.

Signs and Wonders

In the Grasshopper Chapel's early days, pilgrims walked from nearby settlements and often had to wade across the Sauk River to reach Marienberg ("Mary Hill"), near Cold Spring. One little girl and her friends crossed the river at a shallow spot but still got soaked. The little girl worried about her wet, dirty clothes and the scolding she would get from her mother later. When the girls arrived at the top of the holy hill, their dresses and stockings — in a wonder reminiscent of the Miracle of the Sun at Fátima, Portugal — were totally clean and dry!

•••••

Another early story belongs to Mrs. Katharina Hansen and her son, John. While carrying John in her womb, Mrs. Hansen dedicated the child to the Lord's service. When John was eight years old, he was stricken with St. Vitus Dance, a neurological disorder characterized by involuntary twitches and spasms. He lost his ability to walk and talk, and even feeding himself was a challenge. Mrs. Hansen began making pilgrimages to area churches to pray for John's healing. Several months later, the lad showed no signs of improvement.

Mrs. Hansen didn't give up; she was certain John was destined for the priesthood. She undertook yet another pilgrimage, walking barefoot with another son from the family home in Luxemburg to Marienberg, a distance of some fifteen miles. They attended Mass and received Communion, and prayed many Rosaries. When they arrived home several days later, John was fit as a fiddle!

John became a Benedictine priest, taking the name Bonaventure, and served for many years in the Bahamas.

• • • • •

After a tornado blew down the frame chapel in 1894, Marienberg lay in ruins for nearly six decades. One day, a curious visitor looked down into the chapel's foundation hole and saw a perfectly formed cross of small green shrubbery stretching across the hole. The visitor notified Bishop Peter W. Bartholome, of the Diocese of Saint Cloud, who inspected the cross for himself and said, "Rebuild the chapel." It was rebuilt of granite in 1951.

• • • • •

A drinking man left a Cold Spring tavern one night with a pint of whiskey. As he was driving his car out of town, he looked up and saw the brightly illuminated chapel atop the hill. He hit the brakes, turned his car around, and sped back to the tavern. Plunking the pint down on the bar, he bellowed, "Anytime you see a church flying through the air, it's time to quit drinkin'!"

Maria Hilf

Centuries before Maria Hilf drove the locusts out of Cold Spring,

Minnesota, she crushed another plague in Amberg, Germany. As history records, in 1633–34, the Bavarian town was suffering terribly from the bubonic plague, also known as the Black Death. The Grim Reaper was taking up to forty victims per day; entire districts in the town had died out.

In their distress, Fr. Caspar Hell, the Jesuit rector of Amberg, and the townsfolk turned to Our Lady for help and vowed to hold annual pilgrimages if rescue came. They converted a watchtower in the town castle into a chapel for Mary, and on September 3, 1634, Father Hell (German for "bright") led a procession to the hilltop oratory and placed a painting of Maria Hilf inside.

The painting is reportedly a copy of the famous miraculous image by Lucas Cranach the Elder, which now adorns the Cathedral of St. James in Innsbruck, Austria. Unlike that painting, which shows Mother Mary holding the naked Child, her nearly invisible veil covering their foreheads, the painting in Amberg depicts Mother and Child wearing medieval crowns.

The plague immediately subsided and was gone a few months later. The town of Amberg deemed this a miracle, and pilgrims from miles around began descending upon the chapel. In 1641, a larger votive chapel went up. A fire damaged that chapel, but providentially the painting was spared. Today's baroque Wallfahrtskirche Maria Hilf, Pilgrimage Church of Mary's Help, was completed about 1702.

The town never forgot its promise and annually celebrates Mariahilfbergfest, Festival of the Hill of Mary's Help. Held during the week that includes July 2 — the old feast of the Visitation of the Virgin Mary, now celebrated on May 31 — the festival commemorates Mary's "visitation" to Amberg and deliverance from the Black Death.

NEW ULM

Building a church on the frontier took faith — wagonloads of faith. That's the heritage of the **Cathedral of the Holy Trinity** in New Ulm, a German river town in south-central Minnesota. The town is so German the cathedral's Baroque clock tower looks like it might have immigrated with the settlers.

Founded in 1854, New Ulm's early years were beset with trials. Before the Catholic settlers could even finish building their first church, it was destroyed in the US-Dakota War of 1862 — burned by the town's defenders to prevent the Dakota Indians from using it as a barricade. Several years later, the settlers began erecting another house of worship.

Despite living in sod or simple frame houses, the pioneers "spared no expense on their church," wrote John Radzilowski in *Bells Across the Prairie*. Their pastor lived no higher on the proverbial hog. "The simple log parish house had no foundation and the crawlspace underneath the floor provided a fine refuge for an uninvited skunk."

The second church, with a towering steeple, was dedicated in 1870.

Eleven years later, on July 15, 1881, a tornado of F4 magnitude slammed into New Ulm and surrounding area, killing at least twenty people and injuring dozens more. The church roof was blown off and the once-proud steeple reduced to rubble.

Twice humbled, the German flock turned their faces to heaven and pledged to pray the Rosary every Saturday to protect their next church from calamity — a tradition that continues nearly 150 years later.

Clock tower — Cathedral of the Holy Trinity, New Ulm, Minnesota

The third Holy Trinity Church — constructed in 1890 of red brick in Romanesque design and elevated in 1957 as cathedral for the newly created Diocese of New Ulm — is still standing. Now, if that don't beat the devil!

The cathedral is also hailed for its German Baroque interior and titular apse painting (note the zodiac) with cherubim. According to lore, artist Anton Gág modeled the cherubic faces after his own angels: his children. One of those "angels" was Wanda Gág, author and illustrator of the classic children's book *Millions of Cats*.

Come to Mary: 605 North State Street, New Ulm, MN 56073. (507) 354-4158. holycrossafc.org/cathedral-of-the-holy-trinity-history.html.

Iowa

30 **WEST BEND**

When Fr. Paul Matthias Dobberstein made a promise, his word was rock-solid. In June 1897 — a couple of weeks before his priestly ordination — the German native fell gravely ill and was hospitalized. A tenacious sort, Paul pleaded with his doctor to let him be ordained with his class. The doctor relented on one condition: Paul must immediately return to his hospital bed.

Back in hospital, the new Father Dobberstein was diagnosed with double pneumonia. His lungs rattling (back in the day before miracle drugs), he was at death's door. Who doesn't want to live more than a new priest? Father Dobberstein turned to heaven and implored the Blessed Mother to intercede for his life. (It's not known if he invoked Mary under a specific title.)

"For the grace of good health, I will build a grotto in your honor," he vowed, with all the strength he could muster.

Father Dobberstein not only erected his promised grotto, but a composite of nine separate grottos! Dubbed the Eighth Wonder of the World, the **Shrine of the Grotto of the Redemption** in West Bend covers one city block and has a geological value in the millions of dollars. The shrine is more than a tourist attraction, however. It's the captivating tale of a rock hound-spelunker-evangelist who stopped at nothing to tell in silent stone the greatest story on earth.

In October 1898, Father Dobberstein, twenty-six years old, was named pastor of Sts. Peter and Paul Church in West Bend, a German prairie town in north-central Iowa. The Iowa prairie was hardly a hotbed of geological treasures, so he began taking rock-hunting expeditions to South Dakota and Montana and to the Southwest for grotto building material.

Once while gathering calcite in a cave near Sturgis, South Dakota, the spelunker saw tunnels going in many directions and began unrolling a ball of twine string as he went deeper into the cavern. "It would be a return trail," explained Duane Hutchinson in *Grotto Father*.

But Father Dobberstein let go of the string and went exploring. "Lo and behold," continued Hutchinson, "he got lost — couldn't find his way back to the twine string no matter which way he went." The explorer sat tight, until help arrived.

To build his grotto mountain, the priest first had to "move mountains." Some one hundred train-car loads pulled into West Bend loaded with petrified wood, fossils, quartz, Oklahoma barite roses, jasper, turquoise, fool's gold, gypsum, agates as big as a

person's head, shells, coral of every color, and more. Colossal septaria (mud balls) rolled in from North Dakota. James Larkin White, the cowboy who discovered New Mexico's Carlsbad Caverns about 1898 (the caverns were then private property), furnished a one-ton stalagmite.

In West Bend, Father Dobberstein's flock left no stone unturned. Farmers arrived for Sunday Mass with wagonloads of field rock and boulders.

In 1912, after more than a decade of stockpiling, cleaning, and classifying the rocks and minerals — in addition to his parish duties that included a Catholic boarding school — Father Dobberstein began erecting Mary's Grotto. Folks surely gawked as he dug a foundation twenty feet deep (large enough to swallow up a small house!), mixed loads of concrete by hand, scrubbed the farmers' rocks clean, and dumped everything into the abyss.

Then, the artist-priest began setting rocks and semiprecious stones in concrete. Several years in the building, Mary's Grotto "rocks." Creating a Milky Way of sorts, Father Dobberstein hung dozens of rock-stars on the thirty-foot dome ceiling. Over the Star of Bethlehem, he wrote *Ave* upside down. Why upside down? The first *Ave* — meaning *Hail* or *Blessed* — was spoken from heaven, not on earth. More stars encircle a statue of the Blessed Mother and Child.

Nobody knows when Father Dobberstein began envisioning a series of grottos that would tell the Redemption story in stone. But by 1916–17, he had written above Mary's Grotto the words, "Grotto of

Shrine of the Grotto of the Redemption, West Bend, Iowa

the Redemption." From a distance, the faux mountains, with archways and even a rock staircase, resemble an ancient walled-in city. Our Lady is there at nearly every turn — from a medallion of the Immaculate Conception in the Grotto of Paradise Lost, to a recreation of Michelangelo's *Pietà* atop Mount Calvary.

In Father Dobberstein's mind, stones weren't mere stones: Each had a story to tell. A serpent of green stone tempts Eve in Paradise Lost. The Stations of the Cross are done in brown jasper, except for the Twelfth Station (Jesus' death on the cross) done in white rock. "Why the white?" early pilgrims would ask. "Because mankind is now redeemed," the artist explained.

A shroud-draped cross tops Golgotha, a forty-foot mountain peak. Everywhere are stone rosettes for Mary. The artist even started his own stalactites in the Grotto of the Ten Commandments. Most be-gemmed of all? The Christmas Grotto, located inside Sts. Peter and Paul Church, adjacent to the shrine. The magnificent Brazilian amethyst weighs 300 pounds alone.

Decade after decade, Father Dobberstein labored on the monument, aided by his "good right hand," Matthew Szerensce, who began working with him as a lad. The five-foot-six-inch priest even posed for artist sketches of the shrine's sixty-five Carrara marble statues. It's said that when he posed as Judas Iscariot, with a money bag in hand, he felt as mean as the devil.

Age crept up on the grotto builder, and in 1946, newly ordained Fr. Louis H. Greving was sent to West Bend as his assistant. Of German descent, Father Greving spoke German and even looked a bit like Father Dobberstein, albeit taller. Like his superior, Father Greving was a born storyteller.

Father Dobberstein would come up to the rectory for supper, his hands cracked and bleeding from setting rocks in wet concrete, reminisced Father Greving in *Grotto Priest*. "You'd better lay off for a couple of days," he'd tell him.

"There isn't any redemption without a little bit of blood," replied Father Dobberstein. The next day he would be back working.

After forty-two years as grotto builder extraordinaire, Fr. Paul Dobberstein laid down his trowel on July 24, 1954. He was eighty-one years of age. It's no coincidence the Grotto of the Resurrection was his last. Buried with him was the monetary cost of building the shrine; he wanted the cost known to God alone.

The artist often told Father Greving the "show must go on" but left behind no blueprints. Then again, his underling didn't need any. "We had grotto for breakfast, grotto for dinner, and grotto for supper!" Father Greving regaled tourists. "That's how I knew what to do — I had heard it so often."

Father Greving hauled in sixty-five tons of petrified wood from Montana and the Dakotas to finish the Grotto of Bethlehem. As his mentor instructed, he did the interior of the Grotto of Nazareth in white quartz to represent the virtues of a godly home. In 1992, Father Greving erected a larger-than-life bronze statue of Father Dobberstein to honor the grotto founder. In one hand is a pick hammer; in the other, a piece of white quartz.

After fifty-six years of living in the shadow of the world-famous grotto, Father Greving died February 14, 2002, also at age eighty-one.

More than a century has passed since Father Dobberstein built his promised grotto to the Blessed Mother, but the stones still cry out, converting hearts and minds. That's the real miracle of the Shrine of the Grotto of the Redemption — a miracle that will last for all eternity.

Come to Mary: 208 1st Avenue NW, West Bend, IA 50597. (515) 887-2371. westbendgrotto.com.

Signs and Wonders

 Artist. Spelunker. Orator. Son of Mary. Father Dobberstein also had a theatrical side. According to lore, at weddings he would bind the bridal couple with a rope to symbolize their union. Before beginning his long-winded Sunday sermons, he set an alarm clock to signal him when to quit. When the alarm sounded, he knocked the clock on the floor and kept on preaching.

A fisher of men, Father Dobberstein knew that he first needed to reel them in. He excavated a lake, twenty feet deep in places, and stocked it with fish. Then he started a zoo, with a de-scented skunk, peacocks, deer, a bald eagle, and even a caged bear. Tourists came in droves — and so did the converts. In his fifty-six years as pastor, Father Dobberstein signed some 1,000 baptismal certificates.

But nothing captivated tourists and potential converts like his diving stunt. After announcing that he could hold his breath for three minutes, reported Duane Hutchinson in *Grotto Father*, Father Dobberstein would dive into the lake, swim through a culvert to an air space, and linger just long enough for spectators to become frantic and yell for help. Then, wonder of wonders, he would swim back and surface triumphantly!

His little "deaths and resurrections" weren't lost on crowds. They embodied the very message of the Grotto of the Redemption itself — from death to everlasting life.

31 ▶ SIOUX CITY

If you believe in miracles, come to **Trinity Heights Queen of Peace Shrine** in Sioux City. Who else but Mother Mary could have orchestrated this incredible chain of events that turned a forsaken parcel of land in northwestern Iowa into a national Marian shrine — an ecumenical shrine at that? As folks here like to say, "The shrine is no coincidence. It's a 'Mary-incidence!'"

Mary's "miracle spree" in Sioux City began in the early 1980s, when Fr. Harold V. Cooper was visiting the old Trinity High School and College campus, his alma mater. The property began speaking to him: Build a shrine here to Mary.

But what kind of shrine?

The answer came when the priest visited the mega-statue of the Immaculate Heart of Mary at Our Lady of Peace Church in Santa Clara, California (see site 50). The minute he saw the thirty-two-foot stainless steel icon, his mission was clear: Erect a colossal statue of Our Lady on the deserted Trinity campus. There was one "tiny" problem. A real estate developer owned the property and wanted over $300,000. Only heaven had that kind of money.

Father Cooper recruited a small army of Rosary warriors. Every day at 4:00 p.m., Father Cooper, his mother, and others would drive out to the property and pray the Rosary in their cars. "Mary, please make this land available to us, so we may place a statue on this hill in your honor," they petitioned. Month after month, year after year, they prayed their beads.

In 1985, Father Cooper and a lay group formed Queen of Peace, Inc. In an extraordinary leap of faith, the board members left the fundraising to Mary. They would conduct no active fundraising, no fund drives.

"The daily Rosary, each and every day of every year, is our only fundraising effort," wrote Bernard (Beanie) Cooper, former executive director and Father Cooper's younger brother, in *The Miracle of Trinity Heights*. When people asked the priest where the money would come from, he replied, "Mary will take care of that."

Amazingly, unsolicited funds began pouring in.

One day in 1987, Father Cooper got his first miracle. Due to the savings and loan crisis, the Trinity Heights property was now on the market for $93,000 — more than $200,000 less than the original asking price! The board bought the fifty-three acre parcel and commissioned Dale Lamphere, a renowned artist in Sturgis, South Dakota, to sculpt a thirty-foot-tall stainless steel statue of Immaculate Heart of Mary Queen of Peace.

Meanwhile, board members were at an impasse where to place the giant Mary. Some favored the north end of the grounds, others the south end. One day, two board members placed a pole with a white flag halfway between the two ends. The board approved the new location. When the architect began planning the Mound of Mary — a circular base for the statue — he discovered the new location was located directly over the chapel site of the former school. Another Mary-incidence!

The Immaculate Heart of Mary statue, with a halo, was dedicated on June 13, 1993. The daily Rosaries continued.

Then Father Cooper learned Gerald Traufler, a renowned woodcarver in nearby Le Mars, Iowa, was carving a life-size rendition of Da Vinci's *Last Supper*. Rather than modeling the apostles after Da Vinci's

painting, Traufler enlisted friends, family, and even his wife, Arlene, to dress up and pose as the Twelve Apostles. One apostle sports a handlebar mustache, other apostles the hairstyles of the day. You'd have to see the "Apostle Arlene" to believe it! She represents all the women disciples, then and now, of Our Lord, Jesus Christ.

Father Cooper wanted the wooden masterpiece — one of the few life-size Last Suppers in the world — for the shrine. But rumors were flying that a Florida group had offered the postal employee $1 million for the twenty-two-foot-long sculpture. Father Cooper's brother, Beanie, jumped into action and went to visit the artist.

"With more faith than common sense," confessed Beanie, "I offered to build a suitable building" if Traufler placed the massive *Last Supper* at Trinity Heights.

The Rosaries continued, and the carver carved. When Traufler donated the stupendous work of art to Trinity Heights, the board found itself in another holy pickle. Where would they get $285,000 to pay for the promised building? The board proceeded to build in faith and begged Mary's help. When the Saint Joseph Center was about half completed, Father Cooper received a letter. Inside was a check for the exact cost of the center! The Saint Joseph Center and the *Last Supper* were dedicated on Holy Thursday, April 13, 1995.

Not only did Mary deliver a building, but Traufler's *Last Supper* — seven years in the carving — became an ecumenical draw. People of all faiths began

Immaculate Heart of Mary statue — Trinity Heights
Queen of Peace Shrine, Sioux City, Iowa

flocking to Trinity Heights to view the acclaimed sculpture with "Iowa apostles." Some pilgrims weep before the Holy Table: It's the Bible in the vernacular.

The daily Rosaries continued. Up went the Outdoor Cathedral, a church without walls, and the Way of the Saints. The Divine Mercy Chapel was added to the Saint Joseph Center, where the Rosary is now prayed daily at 4:00 p.m. During the COVID-19 lockdown in 2020, the Rosary was broadcast via loudspeakers over the grounds. Pilgrims prayed along in their cars or while socially distancing around the shrine.

As Catholic tradition teaches, the Blessed Mother leads souls to her Son. In 1998, Mega Mary began pointing to a thirty-three-foot stainless steel statue of the Sacred Heart of Jesus, also sculpted by Lamphere. Providentially, when Mary's statue was installed years earlier, her right hand was pointing to the future site of her Son's statue — the altar area in the Outdoor Cathedral. Jesus' footprint may be America's largest: His big toe alone is eighteen inches long! The robes of both statues seem to be blowing in the prairie wind.

What began with the Rosary continues with the Rosary. Only heaven knows what Miracle Mary will do next!

Come to Mary: 2511 Thirty-Third Street, Sioux City, IA 51108. (712) 239-8670. trinityheights.com.

Signs and Wonders
After visiting Trinity Heights Queen of Peace Shrine in Sioux City, one ten-year-old boy remarked, "I feel like I've been to heaven and back." And no wonder. Like Mary's fiat at the Annunciation, the shrine is loaded with "Yes!" stories.

One snowy December day in 1997, a tall man and a short woman walked into the Trinity Heights offices. "Are you planning a shrine to Our Lady of Lourdes?" the seventy-something man asked.

"Yes," said Bernard (Beanie) Cooper, the shrine's executive director.

"How much is that going to cost?"

"Around $50,000," replied Beanie, who related the story in *The Miracle of Trinity Heights*.

The man looked at his wife and said, "I think we can do that. What do you think?"

"We can do that!"

"We've been to Lourdes, France, and to Fátima, Portugal," the man continued. "Are you going to have a shrine to Our Lady of Fátima?"

"Yes, we are," Beanie beamed.

The man looked again at his wife and said, "We can give $50,000 for that one, too."

And so the two shrines came to grace the Trinity Heights grounds. Our Lady of Lourdes appears in a grotto with a trickling stream, and Our Lady of Fátima in a pasture with statues of the shepherd children and sheep.

Other shrines dedicated to Marian apparitions include Our Lady of Mount Carmel, Our Lady of Knock, Our Lady of the Miraculous Medal, and Our Lady of Guadalupe.

Missouri

(32) ► STARKENBURG

There's no trouble too big for the **Shrine of Our Lady of Sorrows** in Starkenburg, a German hamlet set amid rolling hills near Rhineland, west of St. Louis. The troubles here were so bad that Mary came to the settlers' rescue twice! How could she refuse? In Old World tradition, the flock would process around the wooded grounds with their White Lady statue — so named because she was unpainted, or "white."

Like the winding roads in these parts, Our Lady's story takes many twists and turns. In 1847, German Catholics settled the area. Circuit-riding priests would celebrate Mass in a barn, presided over by the White Lady, or *Weisse Dame* in German. Five years later, the settlers built a log church, the White Lady's new home. In 1873, the parish erected Saint Martin's Church of stone and the statue moved again. Some years later, a more elegant Madonna replaced the White Lady, and the old statue was relegated to a church attic.

(Saint Martin's Church is now a church museum, a nineteenth-century timepiece of Catholic artifacts. It looks as though a Latin High Mass could start at any moment.)

In 1887, Fr. George Hoehn arrived as pastor and his nephew, August Mitsch, as sacristan. Mitsch found the White Lady in the attic and, one spring day in 1888, made a May altar for her in a flowering dogwood. The May shrine rekindled the settlers' devotion to the White Lady, and the tiny Log Chapel was built to house her.

Two years later, the White Lady of the Log Chapel got sent back to the attic, supplanted by a small replica of the German sculpture, the Pietà of Achtermann, also known as the Crying Pietà. Farmers were soon weeping with her.

In June 1891, biblical rains began falling over the Starkenburg area. After six weeks of pouring rains, the wheat, literally the people's daily bread, was at stake.

"Mary, save our wheat," the people cried to the Crying Pietà.

Father Hoehn recalled a similar plight in his native Germany when farmers had been caught in a horrific drought. They made a faith-vow to build a chapel to the Mother of God if their prayers for rain were answered. The rains fell, and a chapel was built. If Our Lady heeded that request, the priest reasoned, why wouldn't she perform the opposite miracle and stop the rains?

The Starkenburg parish turned to Our Lady and promised to make annual pilgrimages to the Log Chapel if the rains ceased. The next day dawned sunny and bright! And many days after that. The farmers harvested their wheat, and the first pilgrimage was held that September 8, the feast of the Nativity of the Blessed Virgin Mary.

Three years later, in 1894, the unthinkable happened. A terrible drought prevailed over the land. Crops were doomed. Farmers again rushed to the Log Chapel and wailed, "Mary, please send rain. Spare us our daily bread." They lit candles before the Lady statue, her white veil held in place by a waxen wreath.

During the night of June 24–25, the altar linens caught fire. The wooden altar was charred, but Our Lady escaped harm. Even her veil and waxen wreath

were unscathed. Our Lady not only saved her Log Chapel, but the rains came. Farmers reaped a golden harvest that year.

Word traveled about the "little chapel of miracles," and miracle seekers began visiting here from distant towns. So many pilgrims came that a larger chapel was needed to accommodate them. The Log Chapel was moved some feet away, and a Romanesque Revival chapel of stone erected on that hallowed spot. The Shrine of Our Lady of Sorrows was dedicated on September 15, 1910 — her feast day (see Portland, Oregon, site 49).

And the White Lady? She couldn't be happier! She was brought out of storage, painted in polychrome, and enthroned above the shrine's white marble high altar. Joining her on a side altar is the Crying Pietà. Adding to their mystique, both statues are covered with a sheer white veil, an old German custom.

The Log Chapel, with a mini-apse, stained-glass windows, a bell tower, and a hinged front that opens up like a triptych, wasn't forgotten. Yet another Mary figurine awaits inside to hear pilgrims' problems and woes.

The vowed pilgrimages of the 1890s continue today — on the third Sunday in May and the second Sunday in September — when Our Lady's statues are carried in procession around these holy grounds. More miracles are surely coming this way.

Come to Mary: 197 State Highway P, Rhineland, MO 65069. (573) 236-4390. historicshrine.com.

Shrine of Our Lady of Sorrows, Starkenburg, Missouri

Signs and Wonders

There's no doubting Mary's miracles at the Shrine of Our Lady of Sorrows in Starkenburg. Multiple plaques of thanksgiving line the walls. One plaque, written in German, simply says "Danke" ("Thank you"). A shoe brace tells a healing story at the Lourdes Grotto, also on the shrine grounds. Unlike the original grotto in Lourdes, France, the Starkenburg grotto had no water. So Fr. George Hoehn, the pastor, ordered a well dug and then added blessed water from Lourdes to the well. Thus, the ordinary well water became blessed holy water.

As the story goes, the shoe brace belonged to a young girl who had contracted polio that left one leg shorter than the other. Her parents brought her repeatedly to the Starkenburg grotto and bathed her leg in the holy well water. When no apparent healing came, an operation was scheduled. On the day of surgery, the doctor found nothing wrong with the girl's leg!

Another plaque testifies to another grotto healing. A student noticed a mysterious growth on his hand. He went to the grotto, washed his hands in the holy well water, and prayed. The growth disappeared and never returned. The student later became Msgr. Martin B. Hellriegel, a noted writer of Catholic prayers and hymns, including "To Jesus Christ Our Sovereign King." Written in 1941 in response to the Third Reich's aim of world supremacy, the familiar refrain resounds:

"Christ Jesus Victor, Christ Jesus Ruler!
"Christ Jesus, Lord and Redeemer!"

PORTAGE DES SIOUX

(33)

Our Lady, the Mother of All Peoples, is called by many names. To mariners and fishermen she is none other than Stella Maris (Star of the Sea). In July 1951, the Star of the Sea moved inland and stopped a town from being swallowed up by a sea of a different kind: a flooded river.

Biblical rains were pounding the Midwest that summer. The flooded Missouri River gulped down towns and farmland as it shot across eastern Missouri, where it joins the Mississippi River near Portage Des Sioux. The historic river town was in grave danger of being swept away forever.

Fr. Edward B. Schlattmann, pastor of St. Francis of Assisi Church in Portage Des Sioux, wasn't about to concede defeat to the Big Muddy. He asked the parish Legion of Mary to invoke Mary's protection. As the Legion prayed Rosary after Rosary, the Big Muddy flooded the roads into Portage Des Sioux, turning the town into an island. The only communication with the "mainland" was by boat.

Residents watched in terror as the river crept closer and closer. "For two weeks, the waters going over the fields sounded like the Niagara Falls," stated one account. When the flood finally crested, the town was mostly high and dry. Only one house on the outskirts of town was severely damaged.

The floodwaters parted like the Red Sea, Father Schlattmann told Faith Palmer in *Missouri Life*: "The water, instead of coming down the road like a car would, separated … and went above the town and below the town — not in the town at all." It was a miracle, everyone said.

The town of Portage Des Sioux, located near the confluence of the Illinois, Missouri, and the Mississippi Rivers, wanted to show its gratitude to the heavens above. But how? A plaque at the Catholic church? No, the miracle belonged to everyone. A three-foot statue on the banks of the Mississippi River? A rowboat couldn't see that! This miracle needed something big, really big.

Father Schlattmann hit on the idea of a towering monument to Mary, the mother of all peoples, all races, and all faiths. Surprisingly, everyone — Jews, Catholics, and Protestants — agreed, and Our Lady of the Rivers Shrine was born. Norma McClory of Mattoon, Illinois, was commissioned to sculpt the twenty-five-foot image.

Dedicated in October 1957 — a month devoted to the Most Holy Rosary — this is one unique Mary. Built of fiberglass and standing on a twenty-five-foot base, the white Mary statue has no defined facial features. Because the sunlight bouncing off the river

would create shadows on Mary's face and distort her beauty, the artist made her face soft and simple. Each boater becomes the artist, visualizing in his or her mind Our Lady's face. Her lighted crown serves as a navigational aid for boaters.

Our Lady of the Rivers Shrine is famous for its Blessing of the Fleet and Parade of Boats held each summer. As decorated vessels of all kinds pass by Our Lady, a priest blesses them with holy water and asks heaven's protection on everyone aboard.

Come to Mary: St. Francis of Assisi Church: 1355 Farnham Street, Portage Des Sioux, MO 63373. (314) 482-6084.

Our Lady of the Rivers Shrine: 1553 River View Drive, Portage Des Sioux, MO 63373. ourladyoftheriversshrine.org.

Our Lady of the Rivers Shrine, Portage Des Sioux, Missouri

ST. LOUIS

When the cholera epidemic hit St. Louis in 1849, citizens took to signing their letters "Take care, and don't take the cholera." (Nearly 175 years later, during the COVID-19 pandemic, people took to signing emails and texts, "Take care, and stay safe.") People parting for just a day or two bid farewell as though they wouldn't see each other again. Many times they didn't.

"Often, friends whom I have seen in the morning are lying in their coffins in the evening," Fr. Jean-Pierre De Smet wrote on July 4, 1849, his letters excerpted in *The Life of Father De Smet, S.J.*

The citizenry of St. Louis had good reason to be terrified. An estimated ten percent of the city's population of 70,000 — or 7,000 residents — would die from cholera. At its peak, two hundred funerals were held daily, the incessant tolling of funeral bells casting an invisible pall over the city.

All around St. Louis College, now Saint Louis University, corpses were carried out of homes and stacked in the streets. The rector, professors, and two hundred male student boarders of the Jesuit institution beseeched heaven and bound themselves by a vow to the Blessed Mother.

"We placed ourselves and all our pupils under her powerful protection, promising to adorn her statue with a silver crown should all escape the scourge," Father De Smet wrote in another letter on July 9. "Mary loves her children too well to allow them to perish."

To the city's astonishment, not one student or

"Our Lady of the Plague" statue — St. Francis Xavier College Church, St. Louis, Missouri

faculty member contracted cholera while on campus! Nor did any Jesuit ministering to the sick and
dying. By fall the epidemic had ceased, and in October, the faculty and the student body gathered to
crown a statue of the Blessed Mother and Child,
chiseled of white stone. Tears streamed down their

faces in awe of Mary's munificent love.

"Our Lady of the Plague" stands today in the lower entrance of **St. Francis Xavier College Church**, on the university campus. Some say the blemish at the corner of Mary's mouth is a remnant of the plague, when the skin of cholera victims turned bluish in color. A plaque tells the story of Mary's signal favor. It says, in part: "Their trust in the Divine Mother was gratifying to Her Divine Son, for at Mary's command the deadly plague dared not enter within the walls of the University."

Come to Mary: 3628 Lindell Boulevard, St. Louis, MO 63108. (314) 977-7300. sfxstl.org.

Shrine of Our Lady Queen of Peace — St. John Church, Leopold, Missouri

LEOPOLD

If two strands are stronger than one, imagine the supernatural power of dozens of people praying the Rosary in one accord and with one intention. Parishioners of St. John Church in Leopold don't need to imagine — they know.

During World War II, the good folks of this German-Dutch hamlet, located in southeast Missouri, decided to build an open-air shrine to Our Lady. Everyone, even the children, took to the hills and creek beds to find the "sparkling, quartz-encrusted stones for the walls," wrote Nick J. Elfrink in *101 Inspirational Stories of the Rosary*. Parish men erected the walls and laid the flagstone floor.

In May 1944, the **Shrine of Our Lady Queen of Peace** was dedicated to the safe return of St. John's soldiers at war. Weather permitting, the faith-

ful would gather daily at the shrine around dusk to pray a corporate Rosary for world peace and for loved ones in harm's way. Every one of the parish's forty-four soldiers lived to tell about it!

The Rosary gatherings at the "Shrine of Safe Return" continued during the Korean and Vietnam conflicts. "To this day not one parish member has lost his or her life while serving our country," continued Elfrink. "There were many harrowing tales of near misses, and some men were wounded, but none of the wounds were life-threatening."

The Rosary devotion at St. John Church endures today. Our Lady's prayer warriors gather weekly at the shrine or meet inside the church. On Memorial Day and Veterans Day, flags line the shrine walkway in remembrance of the soldiers who were lifted up here in prayer during the dark days of war. (See Atlanta, Georgia, site 11; St. Benedict, Kansas, site 38; St. Marks, Kansas, site 39; Arapahoe, Nebraska, site 36; Windthorst, Texas, site 45.)

Come to Mary: 103 Main Street, Leopold, MO 63760. (573) 238-3300. stjohnchurchleopold.com.

Nebraska

ARAPAHOE

36

Pray the Rosary and you might save your life. It happened to Fr. Henry Denis, a young Polish priest who escaped death — at least twice — while imprisoned in German concentration camps during World War II. His phenomenal tale of survival is told at **Our Lady of Fatima Shrine**, outside St. Germanus Church, in the small town of Arapahoe.

In 1939, Father Denis, a Polish military chaplain, was taken captive by the Nazis and incarcerated at various concentration camps, including Dachau, from 1942–45. At Dachau, the priest was subjected to Nazi medical experimentation and given a series of malaria injections. According to the *Southern Nebraska Register*, when it came time for his last injections — injections that Father Denis had "witnessed killing all those infected" — he was inexplicably spared. He also survived many days of forced starvation.

A bigger miracle was waiting.

On the morning of October 7, 1944, in retaliation for a prisoner's attempted escape, the Dachau inmates were lined up and randomly selected for execution. "There were many corpses on that day, and all the dead had to be brought and placed in line with those who were alive," recounted Father Denis in historical information provided at the shrine. "There was a lot of shouting, cursing, kicking, and clubbing. One prisoner was missing. Finally, they found him; he was dead.

"To forget that hell on earth, deep in my mind and my heart I prayed the Rosary [using fingers as beads]. The Rosary took me up there, into a different world. There were moments that I did not hear anything."

Later, when the prisoners were sent to their work detail, a German priest-friend asked Father Denis, "Why did they call your name and your number?" Two Polish priests asked him the same. The blood froze in Father Denis's veins. To be called and not report was a Nazi crime punishable by death. Father Denis began preparing himself for execution later that day. When he arrived back at camp, he was astounded that no one was looking for him; the quota of victims had been met. Praying the Rosary had saved his life.

On that day — October 7, the feast of Our Lady of the Rosary — Father Denis vowed to build the Blessed Mother a shrine of gratitude if he survived the hellhole camp.

Months passed, and Father Denis became very

TO THE IMMACULATE MOTHER OF GOD
AND
OUR HEAVENLY MOTHER
OUR LADY OF FATIMA
WITH HOPE AND PRAYER FOR PEACE
REV. HENRY J. DENIS AND HIS FRIENDS OF ALL FAITHS
1956
"E PLURIBUS UNUM"

DONATED BY PALMER BROS.
MELROSE, NEBR.

ill and emaciated. He confided in a German prisoner-priest about his miraculous save and promise to Mary, but doubted that he would live. The priest, with piercing blue eyes, whispered, "You will live. The Americans will liberate us," reported the *Southern Nebraska Register*. "Christ will save a number of priests to give witness to the world. You will be among them. ... Remember Our Lady of Fatima. Spread her message of peace."

The German priest was Fr. Joseph Kentenich, founder of the worldwide Schoenstatt Apostolic Movement, a Marian movement of religious and moral renewal. Just as Father Kentenich predicted, American forces liberated the Dachau camp on April 29, 1945.

After the war, Father Denis fled to Italy and later immigrated to Nebraska at the invitation of Bishop Louis B. Kucera, shepherd of the Diocese of Lincoln. In 1949, Father Denis was named pastor of St. Germanus Church in Arapahoe, in south-central Nebraska, and a mission parish in Oxford.

While Father Denis longed to erect his promised shrine, he first needed to raise funds for church repair. Our Lady even saw to that. As one story goes, on October 7, 1954 — the ten-year anniversary of his providential escape from death — Father Denis celebrated a Mass of thanksgiving. Later that day, a man stopped by the rectory and offered to leave his estate to the parish. The man died shortly thereafter.

As word traveled of the holocaust survivor and his vow to Mary, donations of money, stones, and seashells began arriving from nearly every American state and from Canada and Europe. In August 1956, Father Denis's promise came to pass: Our Lady of Fatima Shrine was dedicated.

In a park-like setting, Our Lady's statue stands high on a pillar, statues of the three shepherd children and animals on shorter pedestals below. Angel statues flank Our Lady. A plaque reads, "To the Immaculate Mother of God and Our Heavenly Mother, Our Lady of Fatima, with hope and prayer for peace, Rev. Henry J. Denis and his friends of all faiths, 1956, E. Pluribus Unum." Another monument honors the American soldiers who liberated Dachau.

In 1999, St. Germanus parish dedicated another statue *Rachel Weeping for Her Children*, memorializing both the victims of the abortion holocaust and children whose lives were tragically cut short. Based on Jeremiah 31:15 and sculpted by Sondra L. Jonson of nearby Cambridge, Nebraska, the larger-than-life bronze statue depicts a sorrowing Rachel kneeling in prayer, her arms cradling an empty blanket. The rose at her side signifies her trust in God and hope for the future.

Commemorating Our Lady of Fatima's plea to pray the Rosary, Jonson also sculpted the four bronze plaques that represent the Joyful, Luminous, Sorrowful, and Glorious Mysteries of the Rosary. (See Atlanta, Georgia, site 11; St. Benedict, Kansas, site 38; St. Marks, Kansas, site 39; and Leopold, Missouri, site 35.)

Come to Mary: 912 Chestnut Street, Arapahoe, NE 68922. (308) 697-3722. arapahoe-ne.com /attractions/shrine.htm.

Signs and Wonders

Our Lady's graces at her shrines never end. When Rhonda Kraft of Liberty, Missouri, lost her teenage daughter in the early morning hours on December 29, 2001, her world stopped. Candace, a high school senior, died in a car accident on the way home from a holiday gathering with friends. Like Rachel of the Old Testament (see Jer 31:15), Rhonda could not be comforted, her child was no more.

One day in March 2002, Rhonda decided to visit Our Lady of Fatima Shrine at Arapahoe, Nebraska. As Rhonda approached the shrine, her car was suddenly, and inexplicably, filled with the fragrance of her daughter's favorite perfume! Heaven comforted a grieving mother that day — a day that will forever live in Rhonda's heart.

Rhonda and family members have visited the shrine many times over the years. On each occasion, they found great comfort and peace in the presence of Our Lady.

Our Lady of Fátima

According to lore, when shepherd children Lúcia dos Santos and cousins Francisco and Jacinta Marto were tending their sheep at the Cova da Iria, near the village of Fátima, Portugal, they often prayed an "expedited" Rosary. They were in a hurry to eat lunch.

"Ave Maria (Hail Mary)," they called out.

"Ave Maria, Ave ... Ave," the hills echoed back.

In no time, their Rosary was finished.

That all changed on May 13, 1917, when Our Lady appeared in a holm oak tree to the little shepherds at the Cova da Iria. Clothed in a dazzling white gown more brilliant than the sun, Our Lady asked Lúcia, age ten, and Francisco and Jacinta, ages eight and seven, to return on the thirteenth day of each month for the next six months. During her apparitions, Mary asked them to pray the Rosary daily (and reverently!) for world peace and to do many penances for the conversion of sinners. Our Lady also revealed her Immaculate Heart (see Sioux City, Iowa, site 31, and Santa Clara, California, site 50) and promised to perform a miracle during her October 13 visit, so that "all may believe."

News of the apparitions spread, and some 70,000 spectators — freethinkers and believers alike — descended upon the Cova da Iria to witness the promised miracle on October 13. Heavy rain began falling and everyone got drenched. Suddenly, the clouds broke and the sun began to spin and dance in the sky! When the spectacle ended, the crowds were flabbergasted to find their wet clothing clean and dry, as though their garments had just returned from the cleaners. The muddy ground under their feet was dry too! This phenomenal event is known as the Miracle of the Sun.

During her October 13 apparition, the Blessed Mother revealed herself to the shepherd children as the Lady of the Rosary. She is more popularly called Our Lady of Fátima.

Our Lady of Fátima is traditionally portrayed wearing a white gown with a white mantle, edged in gold. She wears a crown, her head tilted slightly to her left; her hands, draped with a large rosary, are folded in prayer.

Francisco and Jacinta were canonized on May 13, 2017, the centennial anniversary of Our Lady's first apparition. Lúcia was declared a Servant of God on February 13, 2017.

The feast of Our Lady of Fátima is May 13.

Kansas

ATCHISON

If you doubt the intercessory power of Mother Mary, visit **Benedictine College** in Atchison. It is a college of miracles!

The saga begins in September 1856, when Fr. Henry Lemke, OSB, was walking home one night from a sick call in the prairie wilderness of extreme northeastern Kansas. A torrential thunderstorm struck. Blinded by the pelting rain, the German native lost sight of his navigational guides: trees along the bluffs of the Missouri River. Too many steps in the wrong direction and he would tumble to his death.

Hungry and exhausted, the sixty-year-old priest was lost on the "inland sea," as homesteaders likened the vast prairies with grasses as tall as a man's shoulders. "Because out on these prairies, one is very much like a ship on the ocean which has lost its compass," Father Lemke wrote in *A Warrior in God's Service*. "In my confused state of mind, I was not going to be able to survive the night."

The former Lutheran minister plunged to his knees in the tall grasses and begged the Blessed Mother to rush to his aid. "Up to this point my honoring of Mary had been rather tepid, maybe even cold," confessed Father Lemke. "Yes, I was still a semi-Protestant." But on this night, the convert boldly asked Mary for a sign that she was indeed the "Helper of Christians."

Mary not only sent a sign, but she answered faster than lightning.

As Father Lemke was praying, a young girl asleep in a nearby claim shanty woke up and began to cry. A "lady in white" was standing at the foot of her bed! To calm the girl, the mother lit a lamp and set it in a window. Arising from his knees, Father Lemke saw the light on the horizon and followed it to the shanty, where he took refuge from the deluge.

Convinced the Mother of God had worked a miracle on his behalf, the new "Marian priest" vowed to love and honor her until his last breath.

The next year, Father Lemke founded a Benedictine monastery at Doniphan. In 1858, St. Benedict's Abbey (as the monastery is called today) moved to Atchison, and the monks established St. Benedict's College for men — the same year that a "lady in white" appeared to another young girl, Bernadette Soubirous, at Lourdes, France.

In 1971, St. Benedict's College and Mount St. Scholastica College in Atchison, founded for women in 1923 by Benedictine sisters, merged to form

Benedictine College. The college continues to be cosponsored by the abbey monks and the sisters of Mount St. Scholastica.

Reminiscent of Father Lemke's stormy escapade, Benedictine College in 2007 was in dire need of a swift miracle. According to the college website, enrollment at the four-year liberal arts institution was dropping after having risen above 1,200 students. College president Stephen D. Minnis, imitating St. Teresa of Kolkata who famously prayed the Memorare and obtained spectacular favors from Mary, started a Memorare Army. He enlisted dozens of prayer warriors to pray 1,200 Memorares each to

bolster the college's enrollment.

Mary delivered: 1,232 full-time undergraduate students enrolled for the fall session — many more students than originally projected. A serious student shortfall was averted.

If the Memorare Army worked once, why not again? In 2008, to commemorate the joint 150th anniversary of Our Lady's apparitions at Lourdes and the founding of Benedictine College, the school decided to erect a grotto to honor the "lady in white." President Minnis recruited more warriors to pray 1,000 Memorares apiece to raise the needed funds.

Our Lady came through again.

Located in the heart of campus, Mary's Grotto was constructed of fifty-eight tons of stone, including stones from Lourdes. Blessed water from Lourdes was used to mix the concrete. Dedicated on September 8, 2009, the feast of Mary's birth, the grotto is illuminated at night, harkening back to the miraculous light that saved Father Lemke's life in that deadly prairie storm.

Other Marian tributes on campus include a twenty-one-foot fountain statue of Our Lady of Grace and a Rosary Walk, the inlaid beads filled with blessed Miraculous Medals.

Come to Mary: 1020 North Second Street, Atchison KS 66002. (800) 467-5340. benedictine.edu.

Signs and Wonders

Sometimes miracles happen right before our eyes.

On September 8, 2009, Archbishop Joseph F. Naumann of the Archdiocese of Kansas City, Kansas, was slated to dedicate Mary's Grotto at Benedictine College in Atchison. The ceremony would begin with a 5:00 p.m. Mass in St. Benedict's Abbey church, adjacent to the college, followed by a procession to the outdoor grotto for the blessing and dedication. But at 3:00 p.m. that afternoon, it was pouring rain at the chancery offices in Kansas City, and meteorologists were predicting rain for the Atchison area well into the evening.

Archbishop Naumann telephoned Steven D. Minnis, president of Benedictine College, and asked him to rally his Memorare Army to storm heaven for good weather. For the next two hours, the army prayed, "Remember, O most gracious Virgin Mary, that never was it known that anyone who fled to thy protection, implored thy help, or sought thine intercession, was left unaided."

On the archbishop's fifty-mile drive to Benedictine College later that afternoon, the rain continued right to the Atchison city limits, when it stopped. "Yet, the skies looked ominous," wrote Archbishop Naumann in a 2010 column for *The Leaven*, the archdiocesan newspaper. "I feared that by 6:00 p.m., the time for the blessing of the grotto, Atchison would also be enveloped in rain."

When the procession left the abbey church for the grotto, the sun was shining — perfect weather to bless a grotto! It did not start raining in Atchison until 9:00 p.m., well after the festivities were over.

Coincidence? Maybe not. As it so happened, continued the archbishop's column, a college staff member was in Kansas City the night of the dedication. The man struck up a conversation with an air traffic controller about the weather and how the storm surely dampened the grotto ceremony. What really transpired is nothing short of a miracle.

According to the air traffic controller, the storm system had been advancing at a steady clip over Kansas when it mysteriously stalled at 4:00 p.m., just outside of Atchison. Around 9:00 p.m., the storm kicked in again and moved on.

Mary had cleared the weather for the dedication!

 ## Our Lady of the Memorare

One of the biggest believers in the ancient Memorare (Latin for "Remember") prayer was St. Teresa of Kolkata. Whenever she had a need — and she had oodles of them — she flew to Jesus through the intercession of his Mother.

One day, Mother Teresa, foundress of the Missionaries of Charity, needed $85,000 to buy a building. She asked her Sisters to pray 85,000 Memorares — one Memorare for each dollar needed. When the prayers had been said, a man walked in off the street and handed her a check for $85,000.

In 1984, Mother Teresa, a number of her religious sisters, and throngs of pilgrims were gathered in St. Peter's Square to attend an outdoor Mass offered by Pope St. John Paul II. Rain was coming down in sheets. Mother Teresa instructed her sisters to pray a "flying novena" of ten Memorares for beautiful weather. (Nine Memorares for the petition, and a tenth Memorare as thanksgiving in advance for favor received.) During the first two Memorares, it began raining even harder. By the time the sisters had finished the ninth Memorare, the pilgrims were closing their umbrellas.

Whether in a flying novena, or a novena of 85,000 prayers, the seventy-three word Memorare is quick and efficacious:

> Remember, O most gracious Virgin Mary,
> That never was it known that anyone
> who fled to thy protection,
> Implored thy help or sought thine intercession was left unaided.
> Inspired by this confidence, I fly unto
> thee, O Virgin of virgins, my Mother.
> To thee do I come, before thee I stand,
> sinful and sorrowful.
> O Mother of the Word Incarnate, despise
> not my petitions,
> But in thy mercy hear and answer me.
> Amen.

38 ST. BENEDICT

In 1936, Fr. Cyril Bayer, OSB, prophesied to his parishioners at St. Mary's Church in tiny St. Benedict, "I promise you something wonderful if you build a grotto to Our Lady of Lourdes." According to parish history, **St. Mary's Grotto** was started that November 1, All Saints Day.

With rocks picked on area farms, the young parish men erected an apse-like cavern on the church grounds in this blink-and-you'll-miss-it hamlet in the northeastern corner of Kansas. Measuring about twenty-six feet wide and fifteen feet deep, the grotto is embellished with a curved arch and stony pinnacles. A statue of Our Lady of Lourdes stands on a rock ledge, and a Bernadette statue kneels on the cave floor. Reminiscent of a church sanctuary, steps lead up to the grotto opening.

Five years later, on December 7, 1941, America entered World War II. Some sixty parish men — many of the same men who had helped build the grotto — left to fight the Axis Powers in Europe and the Pacific. Nobody knew if or when they would see their loved ones again.

Father Bayer and his flock also went to war — spiritual war. Every evening after the farm chores were done, they would gather at the grotto to recite the Rosary and other prayers, imploring Mary to cover their soldiers with her mantle of protection. In inclement weather, they prayed inside the prairie church, so breathtakingly beautiful it's heralded as one of the 8 Wonders of Kansas Art.

Year after year, the Rosary warriors entreated

St. Mary's Grotto, St. Mary's Church, St. Benedict, Kansas

Our Lady. Only heaven knows their many tears that watered the grotto grass.

Just as Father Bayer predicted, something wonderful happened. Not one "St. Benedict boy" died in combat! Nearby Frankfort, Kansas, with a population of around 1,200 at the time, "lost thirty-two men during the conflict," reported Marc and Julie Anderson in *The Leaven*, a publication of the Archdiocese of Kansas City, Kansas. St. Mary's parishioners "credited the men's safety to the intercession of the

Blessed Virgin."

More parish men were called up to fight in the Korean and Vietnam wars. Once again, prayer warriors gathered at the grotto on bended knee. Again, something wonderful happened: Not one of their soldiers died in either conflict.

The "miracle grotto" is more than church history, however. Parishioners still meet at the grotto during the summer months to ply their beads, and hardly a day goes by that pilgrims and tourists don't stop to marvel at the wonder of it all. (See Atlanta, Georgia, site 11; St. Marks, Kansas, site 39; Leopold, Missouri, site 35; Arapahoe, Nebraska, site 36; Windthorst, Texas, site 45).

Come to Mary: 9208 Main Street, St. Benedict, KS 66538. (785) 336-3174. stmarystbenedict.org.

ST. MARKS

39

When the Second World War broke out, Msgr John Hackenbroich launched a Marian tradition at St. Mark the Evangelist Catholic Church in St. Marks, a German hamlet near Colwich. The old German priest led the congregation in reciting the Rosary before Sunday Mass for parish servicemen at war and ending Mass with the rousing singing of the hymn "Mary, Help Our Valiant Soldiers."

Our Lady valiantly brought all forty-seven soldiers home — alive. "Several had been badly wounded; some had been decorated for their valor; one had spent some time as a prisoner of war in Germany," reported Brenda M. Eck in *The Catholic Advance*. "But all had survived."

Forever grateful to Mary, the parish erected **Our Lady of Lourdes Grotto** just outside the 1903 Romanesque stone church. Constructed of petrified wood, quartz, field rock, granite, limestone from the Flint Hills of Kansas, and more, the shrine exudes an otherworldly peace. A statue of Our Lady stands in a rocky alcove at the top of the grotto, a kneeling Bernadette statue looks up at her in wonder. Below the alcove, a stone tablet is engraved with the names of all forty-seven soldiers and the Latin words "Deo Gratias" ("Thanks be to God") and "Ave Maria" ("Hail, Mary").

During the Korean and Vietnam conflicts, more sons of St. Mark's went off to fight. "Again, the parish offered the Rosary for their safe return," continued Eck. "Again, several were wounded. Again, all survived."

Stepping into Monsignor Hackenbroich's spiritual shoes, parishioners take turns leading the Rosary before daily and weekend Masses. A Rosary is also

prayed every Sunday evening (weather permitting, the Rosary is held outdoors at the grotto) for the protection of our nation. (See Atlanta, Georgia, site 11; St. Benedict, Kansas, site 38; Leopold, Missouri, site 35; Arapahoe, Nebraska, site 36; and Windthorst, Texas, site 45.)

The prairie church is also known for its turn-of-the-twentieth-century ambiance. Relics include the German stained-glass windows (the "Hl" isn't text speak for "hello," but the German abbreviation for "saint"); three ornate circles on the nave ceiling from which hung Coleman lanterns before the church added electricity in 1933; and the clock tower with Stars of David, an early Christian symbol for Mary.

Come to Mary: 19230 W. Twenty-ninth Street N., Colwich, KS 67030. (316) 796-1604. stmarkks.org.

Our Lady of Lourdes Grotto, St. Mark the Evangelist
Catholic Church, St. Marks, Kansas

MOUNTAIN WEST

Pacific
Ocean

Columbia

90

84

★ Boise

5

80

Grea
Sal
Lak

● Reno
★ Carson City

15

● Las Vegas

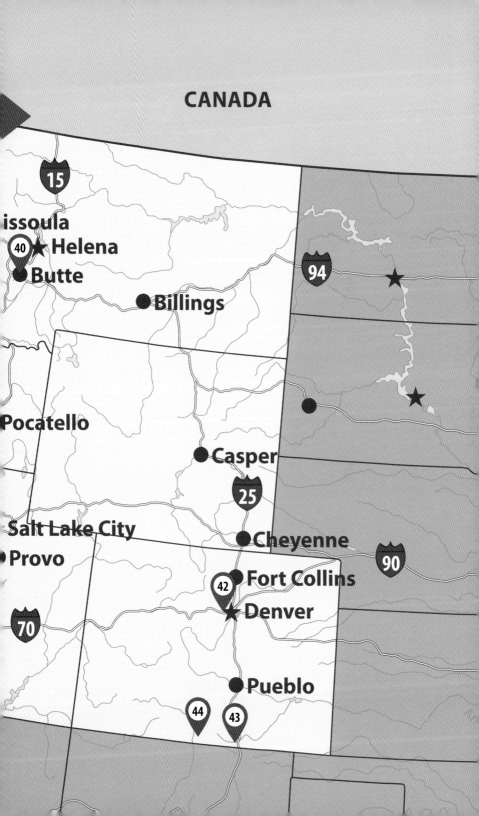

CANADA

15

issoula
40 ★ Helena
● Butte

● Billings

94

★

Pocatello

●

Casper

25

Salt Lake City
● Provo

● Cheyenne

90

70

42 ● Fort Collins
★ Denver

● Pueblo

44   43

Montana

40 ▶ **BUTTE**

When you make a promise to Our Lady, don't be surprised if she takes over. She certainly did with **Our Lady of the Rockies** — America's third tallest statue — which sits atop the Continental Divide overlooking the city of Butte. As local residents were apt to say, "What Our Lady wants, Our Lady gets!" — even if she needed to work a string of miracles to bring it to pass.

The monumental story begins in December 1979 with Bob O'Bill, a Butte resident. According to lore, O'Bill's wife, Joyce, needed cancer surgery and was given a fifty percent chance of survival. As his wife went under the knife, O'Bill, an electrician, was "wiring" heaven: He vowed to erect a five-foot statue of Mary in their yard if Joyce lived. She did.

Within a day, O'Bill's promise had snowballed into a sixty-foot icon that would stand on the East Ridge of the Rocky Mountains, just east of Butte. He met with friends and local businessmen to discuss the idea.

"Why not make the statue ninety feet tall?" they asked. "That way all of Butte can see her." Two of the men gave $1,000 each to launch the project.

Then the miracles began. The land for the statue, blasting powder, the use of heavy equipment to cut a road up the mountain, the sand and cement for the concrete base, tons of steel, umpteen gallons of white paint — all donated. Machine operators, tradesmen, an engineer, and many others volunteered their time and expertise. Cash donations paid for the rest. Our Lady even provided a place in Butte to build the statue: Roberts' Rocky Mountain Equipment Company. Owner Joe Roberts was one of the statue's biggest promoters.

One day, Roberts gave employee LeRoy Lee, a welder, a task that would change his life. "You're going to sculpt a statue of Mary," he told Lee.

"Who, me?" Lee asked. A high school dropout, Lee was an accomplished welder but hardly a sculptor. Lee built a finger — five feet long. The finger became an eight-foot hand. The Virgin's gigantic face proved a far greater challenge, however. After working on the face for three days without success, Lee was ready to quit.

"I'm no sculptor," the doubting welder told his wife.

That weekend at Mass, Lee glanced up at a statue of Mary and the Baby Jesus. "Being a convert, I had never said a prayer to Mary," wrote Lee in *Our Lady Builds a Statue*. "When I did pray, it was always to God." But that day, Lee felt compelled to talk directly to Mary. "Mary, if you want me to build a statue of you, you have to help me," Lee told her.

The answer for the Virgin's face came that night in a vision, as though Lee were watching a movie of himself creating the face and how to do it. When Lee got to work on Monday morning, the face took shape just as he had been shown. He no longer doubted the intercessory power of Our Lady.

Meanwhile, Butte — once a mining boomtown and a leading copper producer — was mired in a severe economic depression. Mines had shut down, jobs were scarce, and morale in the multiethnic town had hit rock bottom. Butte was on its knees.

Ironically, because so many workers were laid off, they had to time to work on the monument. Soon the town began saying, "When the statue of Our Lady goes up on the mountain, Butte will turn around." The statue became an icon of hope.

Lee and fellow workers continued welding, turning iron and rolled plate steel into a colossal work of art. Mary's neck and shoulders were fashioned, her veil went on. Section by section — six sections in all — Our Lady came to life. Then she was painted a pearlized white.

In September 1985, while the 425-ton concrete base for the statue was being poured, heaven intervened again. As dark storm clouds rolled in, they would inexplicably separate — half of the clouds veering south, the other half to the north. "It would rain on both sides of us, but not a drop on the mountain while we were making the pour," continued Lee.

Three months later, on December 17, Mary was assumed into Montana heaven. Manned by a crew from the Nevada National Guard, a Sikorsky Sky-

Our Lady of the Rockies, Butte, Montana

crane helicopter flew the bottom two sections of Our Lady's humongous dress to the site. Two more sections — 17,000 pounds and 19,000 pounds — flew up the following day. On December 19, while the upper extremity was being set in place, Our Lady's right hand was damaged, causing one finger to cross over another — just like the crossed fingers of the townsfolk listening by radio below.

On December 20 — six years after O'Bill made his promise to Mary — the statue's head was airlifted and mounted atop her colossal body. Our Lady was home, her arms and hands open wide, as though she were dispensing graces and miracles on the town below. The economy of Butte began to rebound, just as the people believed it would. Despair turned to joy.

Later, the statue was also dedicated to "all women, especially mothers." Pilgrims and tourists can walk inside the statue and leave a plaque or rosary in memory of a family member or loved one.

Illuminated at night, Our Lady of the Rockies is visible from Interstates I-25 and I-90, a beacon of hope to passersby that everything — even a miracle — is possible with prayer. When a full moon rises behind the statue, the celestial Lady appears out of this world.

Come to Mary: 3100 Harrison Avenue (Butte Plaza Mall), Butte, MT 59701. (406) 782-1221. Only authorized tours and pilgrimages are allowed on the mountaintop site. ourladyoftherockies.com.

Signs and Wonders

Ranked among the world's ten tallest statues of Mary — Mother of All Asia, Tower of Peace in Batangas City, Philippines, takes top honors at 322 feet — Our Lady of the Rockies boasts some impressive statistics of her own:

- Height: Ninety feet
- Weight: Fifty-one tons
- Width: Forty-eight feet
- Head: Eleven by sixteen feet
- Eyes: Three feet wide each
- Hands: Eight feet long and weighing 300 pounds each
- Elevation: 8,150 feet above sea level on the Continental Divide

Many mystical stories are told of Our Lady of the Rockies. As people gaze upon Our Lady, she seemingly looks back on them. Some airline passengers claim her head moves and follows their plane, as though she is guiding them safely into the Butte airport. Motorists on the Interstates below report a great sense of peace and joy as they drive past the Lady. Pilgrims to the holy mountain feel the weight of life melt away in her presence.

And why not?

Our Lady's statue was born of a miracle!

STEVENSVILLE

Highly favored is **Historic St. Mary's Mission** in Stevensville. Founded in 1841 and touted as where the "State of Montana Began," the mission boasts many firsts: one of Montana's first cattle branding irons (a cross atop a semicircle), the first "drive-through pharmacy" (a log cabin with a window where remedies were dispensed), and the first grist and saw mills. But St. Mary's has an even bigger claim: Our Lady appeared to a Salish Indian boy and taught him his prayers!

It was Christmas Eve 1841, and the boy was having great difficulty learning his prayers so he could be baptized on Christmas Day with the other Salish, also called the Flatheads. According to Jesuit Father Jean-Pierre De Smet in *Origin, Progress, and Prospects of the Catholic Mission to the Rocky Mountains*, the mother scolded the boy and said, "The Great Spirit will be angry with you, and will never admit you into heaven if you do not learn your prayers."

"Mother," the boy answered, "the Great Spirit will take pity on me — I tried to learn my prayers and I have been unable to do it. However, I will go again and try."

The boy, around eleven years old, set off to the lodge of a catechist. When he opened the flap, he found a very beautiful lady, her garments white as snow, standing two feet off the ground! Over her head was a bright star; under her feet, a half moon and a serpent, with a strange fruit in its jaws. Rays of light from her visible heart beamed down upon him. The boy fell to his knees and begged the Lady to teach him his prayers. Suddenly, his mind cleared, his heart warmed, and he instantly knew all his prayers.

The boy ran back to his tipi and "told his mother he knew his prayers," continued Father De Smet. "She could not believe it — he recited them in her presence, and knew them so accurately, that he corrected his sister, who mistook in two or three words."

It was a Christmas miracle — of infused knowledge!

When Father De Smet and others questioned the boy about the Lady, his story never wavered, not one jot.

The boy was baptized on Christmas Day, along with 150 other Indians, and given the Christian name Paul (he was called "Little Paul" to differentiate him from "Big Paul," the Salish Chief). Later, a wooden statue of the Blessed Mother was enthroned on a pedestal at the apparition site and aptly called Our Lady of Prayer. The children would pick wildflowers for the Lady.

Christmas Eve wasn't Our Lady's only visit to Little Paul, who died two years after being baptized. She also appeared to him in his dreams. One time, the Lady told him that she was pleased the first Salish mission was named St. Mary.

And therein lies more mystical intrigue. Some months before the Black Robes (the Indian name for the Jesuits who wore black cassocks) arrived here, a band of Salish were encamped in the valley. A girl fell gravely ill and asked to be baptized. A Christian Iroquois Indian named Pierre, who had been adopted into the Salish tribe, baptized the girl and gave her the name Mary.

According to Father De Smet who heard the story from the Salish, Little Mary cried out, "O! there is no happiness in this world — happiness is only to be found in heaven. I see the heavens opened, and the Mother of Jesus Christ inviting me to go up to heaven." Turning to her astonished tribe, Little Mary added, "Listen to the black-gowns when they come — they have the true prayer — do all they tell you — they will come — and on this very spot where I die, they will build the house of prayer!"

With that, her spirit flew to heaven.

So it came to pass that St. Mary's Mission, in the shadow of the Bitterroot Mountains in western Montana, was founded by Black Robes on September 24, 1841. One mountain peak was named Saint Mary, another peak, Saint Joseph.

The first log chapel, twenty-five by thirty-three feet, boasted two galleries and could hold the entire tribe. As news of Little Paul's miracle circulated, many Indians from other tribes were instructed in the faith and baptized here. It was the first church revival in Montana!

When the Kalispel Indians learned of the Black Robes at St. Mary's Mission, they sent an "intelligent young Indian, possessing excellent memory, to visit the Flatheads," wrote Lucylle H. Evans in *St. Mary's in the Rocky Mountains*, a fascinating read of the mission's first years. "He learned the prayers, hymns, and the great truths of the Catholic religion and, upon his return, was made the apostle of the tribe. His instructions were handed from one lodge to another, and before the winter was over more than half the tribe was Christian."

St. Mary's Mission built a larger church. In 1846, a third, and even larger, structure was begun. However, hostile attacks by another Indian nation forced the mission to close. The property was sold

Log church built in 1866, Historic St. Mary's Mission, Stevensville, Montana

in 1850 and became Fort Owen, a trading post, now Fort Owen State Park. The church was intentionally burned to prevent its desecration.

The Blessed Mother didn't forget the Salish. In 1866, Fr. Joseph Giorda, Jesuit superior for the Rocky Mountain area, reestablished St. Mary's Mission, about a mile south of Fort Owen. A log chapel went up, and the mission became the Jesuit provincial headquarters.

Italian born and a "Jesuit-of-all-trades," Fr. Antonio Ravalli — the state's first physician, surgeon, and pharmacist who had previously served at the mis-

sion — was recalled to the Bitterroot Valley. A true Renaissance man, Father Ravalli had an artistic flair and turned the log chapel into a pioneer cathedral. He painted the interior with the colors of the earth, using vermillion clay for the reds, blue from indigo traded among the Indian tribes, and yellow from a cave along the Judith River.

The artist often had to improvise and use whatever resources were at hand, even making "his paint brushes of hair from the tail of his favorite cat," noted Evans. The baptismal font was crafted from tin cans.

Father Ravalli turned a pine log into a Mary statue, her robe tinted blue with berry juice, and fashioned a crucifix from the handle of a shepherd's crook. He created a Black Robe effigy of Saint Ignatius, a founder of the Jesuit order, dressing an iron frame in canvas "dyed" with black tar and paint. The saint's head and hands are carved wood, but his shoes, belt, and rosary are the real deal.

The large, captivating painting of Our Lady's apparition to Little Paul on Christmas Eve is the work of another Jesuit artist: Br. Joseph Carignano. Little Paul kneels before Mary, rays from her heart beaming down on him. (Father Ravalli's painting of the miraculous event graces the rectory of St. Francis Xavier Church in nearby Missoula, Montana.)

St. Mary's Mission closed again in 1891, when the Salish were forced to move to the Flathead Indian Reservation, seventy miles away. The mission was reopened in 1921 and served as the parish church of Stevensville until 1954, when the present St. Mary's Mission Church was dedicated. Stained glass recreates the story of Montana's first Catholic church.

A national historic (and spiritual) site, St. Mary's Mission and Museum includes the 1866 log church, enlarged in 1879, with attached residence; Father Ravalli's cabin and pharmacy; Chief Victor's cabin-turned-Salish-museum; burial grounds; and the old dove cote.

Come to Mary: Historic Saint Mary's Mission: 315 Charlos Street, Stevensville MT 59870. (406) 777-5734. saintmarysmission.org.

St. Mary's Church: 333 Charlos Street, Stevensville, MT 59870. (406) 777-5257. stmarymissionchurch .org.

Signs and Wonders

Nearly two decades before the Blessed Mother appeared to Little Paul at St. Mary's Mission, the Gospel arrived in the Bitterroot Valley of western Montana with some unique evangelists: Iroquois Indians. In 1823–24, twelve Iroquois, employed as fur trappers with the Hudson's Bay Company of Ontario, were trapping in the area and decided to remain with the Salish. The tribe adopted the Iroquois, whose Indian nation had been Christianized by the Jesuits some two hundred years earlier.

The Iroquois, in particular Big Ignace, began telling the Salish about the Jesuits who wore black robes, carried crucifixes, and promised life after death. The Salish and the Nez Perce Indians became so enamored with this God that they dispatched four separate delegations to St. Louis, Missouri, to get Black Robes to come teach them.

The first delegation of seven departed in late summer of 1831. When the group arrived at Council Bluffs, Iowa, three Indians returned home. The other four continued and arrived in St. Louis around October 1. All four fell gravely ill; two died and were buried in the old cathedral cemetery.

According to Lucylle H. Evans in *St. Mary's in the Rocky Mountains*, "When two priests called on them they gave evidence of their knowledge of the Catholic faith by fervently seizing the crucifix shown them and holding it with such tenacity that it was taken away only after death."

But no Black Robes were available, and the two remaining Indians left St. Louis. One died on the way home, and the other was later killed in battle.

In late summer of 1835, Big Ignace and his two sons, ages ten and fourteen, set out for St. Louis, arriving in late fall. Big Ignace cried tears of joy when the Black Robes baptized his sons, Charles and Francis Xavier. Again, no Black Robes could be spared, and the party returned home.

Two years later, in the summer of 1837, a third expedition was sent forth, with Big Ignace again as leader. All five were massacred en route to St. Louis.

Amazingly, the Salish didn't lose faith; in 1839, they sent a fourth delegation. This time they met with success. Fr. Pierre-Jean De Smet, along with two Jesuit priests and three Jesuit brothers, arrived in the Bitterroot Valley on September 24, 1841, the feast of Our Lady of Mercy, and named the new mission St. Mary's.

Exactly three months later, on December 24, Our Lady visited Little Paul in a tipi and granted him a miracle of infused knowledge. Word of the supernatural event spread like a forest fire to other Indian tribes, and many hundreds of Indians were baptized in the Faith.

 ## Our Lady of the Christmas Star

When Fr. Jean-Pierre De Smet questioned Little Paul about Our Lady's apparition on Christmas Eve 1841, he showed the boy an image of the Immaculate Conception. "He recognized her immediately, with this difference, that he saw her only with one star, with her hands joined before her breast, and with her heart visible," wrote Father De Smet in *Origins, Progress, and Prospects of the Catholic Mission to the Rocky Mountains.* "The circumstance of the single star coincided singularly with the festival of Christmas."

On Christmas Day, Father De Smet baptized 150 Salish Indians, including Little Paul. The words of the hymn *Joy to the World* never rang truer than on that wondrous day at St. Mary's Mission in Montana's Bitterroot Valley. In the shadow of Saint Mary's Peak and Saint Joseph's Peak, the Savior had come to the Salish.

Colorado

GOLDEN

42

You might call the **Mother Cabrini Shrine**, near Golden, the "Lourdes of Colorado." In September 1912, several Missionary Sisters of the Sacred Heart of Jesus told Mother Frances Cabrini, who founded the religious order in 1880, that they needed fresh water. Water to drink, water to wash in. According to tradition, the future saint said, "I say a spring has to be here."

But was there? In 1909 when the Italian native bought the first parcel of land — on the east slope of Lookout Mountain —as a summer camp for her girls at the Queen of Heaven Orphanage in Denver, it was dirt cheap. It was said that no water could be found on the land. Water for drinking and cooking had to be hauled up from a stream at the bottom of a canyon.

Mother Cabrini walked around the property and then tapped a large red rock with her cane,

chronicled Mother Ignatius Miceli, MSC, in *Cabrinian Colorado Missions*. "Dig a small hole, for beneath this rock is water fresh and light that all can drink, a marvelous mineral water," the sixty-two-year-old missionary instructed her thirsty sisters. Reminiscent of Bernadette at Lourdes, the sisters turned the rock over and dug a small hole. Water began trickling out of the ground! The miraculous spring is still running today. Similar to Lourdes, many cures have been reported here, even an archbishop's stomach ailment.

In 1927, Jean Baptiste Pitaval, archbishop emeritus of the Archdiocese of Santa Fe, spent ten days here and drank daily of the spring. According to Mother Miceli, the prelate claimed the spring was better than the world-famous Vichy waters of his native France. "My digestion has bothered me for seventy years, but while drinking this water, it has not bothered me at all," he told the sisters.

In 1912, Mother Cabrini also prophesied, "I can envision many small chapels here where many pilgrims will come to pray." Her words came to pass. In addition to the blessed spring, which feeds into an 8,000-gallon tank where pilgrims may drink of the water or bottle it to take home, the picturesque grounds include the Grotto Chapel, the 373-step Stairway of Prayer to the Mount of the Sacred Heart (the view is worth the penance!), and the Cabrini Museum.

Come to Mary: 20189 Cabrini Boulevard, Golden, CO 80401. (303) 526-0758. mothercabrinishrine.org.

Aerial view — Mother Cabrini Shrine, Golden, Colorado

TRINIDAD

Many legends are told the world over of people finding a statue or icon of the Blessed Mother in the most unusual places. In crooks of trees; bobbing on a board in the deep blue sea (see Miami, Florida, site 13); hidden in caves. The **Ave Maria Shrine** in Trinidad, a Wild West town in southern Colorado, began with a mysterious light on a snowy hill.

In 1908, a Trinidad physician was leaving old Mt. San Rafael Hospital in the early dawn hours. A blizzard was raging, but the doctor, tired from all-night duty, climbed into his horse and buggy and headed for home. Suddenly, he saw a light on a hill near the hospital. A light in a snowstorm? It must be an optical illusion created by the snow, he reasoned.

But the thought of someone hurt or stranded in the storm compelled him to stop. The good doctor got out of his buggy and followed the light up the steep, slippery slope. In a clearing at the top, he found a 250-pound statue of Mary, a flickering candle at her feet! Was the statue for real? He touched Mary's outstretched hand — the statue was real. He began calling out, "Is anybody here?" But no answer came. The doctor took refuge by Our Lady until daybreak.

How did the statue get there? Nobody knows, but one title for Mary is Our Lady of Light.

In 1934, the Circolo Mariano (Circle of Mary), a local group devoted to Mary, built the Ave Maria Shrine, a gleaming white Spanish-style chapel on the hilltop site. In 1962, vandals attacked Mary's statue — reportedly the same statue the doctor found on the hill — and smashed it into 279 pieces. Our Lady

"Behold your Mother" (Jn 19:27) — Our Lady's outstretched hands remind us of her maternal care

didn't vanish from sight, however. Sam Arguello and his son Anthony restored the statue, piece by painstaking piece. Our Lady's statue, her scars visible for all to see, stands in a place of honor above the altar.

An enormous blue rosary adorns the façade, while two Our Lady of Grace statues greet pilgrims at the bottom of a staircase to the shrine. A sign on the grounds reads, "God grants Amazing Graces to those who Honor Mary."

Come to Mary: 412 Benedicta Avenue, Trinidad, CO 81082. (719) 846-3369. Call ahead for shrine access. trinidadcatholic.org.

CONEJOS

Our Lady chose the site for the Basilica of Our Lady of Guadalupe in Mexico City. According to lore, she also picked the site for Colorado's oldest parish: **Our Lady of Guadalupe Church** in Conejos, a hamlet in high desert country just over the New Mexico line. (San Acacio Mission Church, built about 1860, in nearby Viejo San Acacio, is hailed as Colorado's oldest standing church.)

In 1854, Hispano settlers from northern New Mexico were traveling through the area when one of the burros in the pack train balked. Nothing, not beatings nor coaxing, could make the stubborn beast go. So, the men decided to lighten the burro's load, stated Aaron Abeyta in "The Burro Story." Still, the beast refused to budge.

"It was not until the contents of the panniers were unpacked that a small statue of La Virgen de Guadalupe was found amongst the other possessions," wrote Abeyta. The settlers took this as a sign and vowed to build the Virgen a church on that very spot. The burro balked no more and trotted along with the rest of the pack train.

True to their word, the pioneers built a primitive church on the north bank of the Conejos River and called their settlement Guadalupe. Due to flooding, they erected a jacal (picket) church, about 1857, on higher ground on the opposite side of the river. A few years later, a larger adobe church to Our Lady of Guadalupe was built over and around the jacal. When the new church was finished, the jacal was torn down and carried out the front doors of the

Painting with "crown of soot" — Our Lady of Guadalupe Church, Conejos, Colorado new church.

A fire on Ash Wednesday 1926 claimed that house of God, and today's picturesque church, in Spanish Colonial Revival design, went up.

Ninety years later, another fire broke out on Ash Wednesday Eve in 2016. Providentially, parishioner Jimmy Atencio, Junior, was passing by the church and saw smoke coming from the inside. As it so happened, local firefighters were gathered for a meeting at the firehouse in Antonio, three miles down the

road, when the 911 call came in. The volunteer fire-fighters were on the scene within minutes, and Our Lady's church was saved.

But the fire left behind smoke damage and a mystical image created by soot — a multi-pointed crown on a large portrait of Our Lady of Guadalupe over the high altar (see Santuario de Guadalupe in Santa Fe, New Mexico, site 48). The crown rests on her head, just like it belongs there. Mary is Queen of Heaven and Earth, after all.

The crown of soot is still visible today.

Dubbed "A Place of Miracles," Our Lady of Guadalupe Church is known for another unique Marian attraction: A huge labyrinth with six-foot-tall adobe walls. (Parishioners made the tens of thousands of adobe bricks the old-fashioned way — by hand, just like their ancestors before them.) The walls not only encircle the shrine but form the tunnel-like walkway inside. Once you set foot inside the labyrinth, measuring 135 feet in diameter, you're on a pathway into Mary's very own heart. Niches with bas relief plaques depict the twenty Mysteries of the Rosary.

Welcoming pilgrims are bronze statues of Our Lady of Guadalupe and Juan Diego.

Erected in honor of the Hispano pioneers, El Santuario de los Pobladores ("The Sanctuary of the Settlers") is expected to be completed in 2023. If you visit on an adobe-making day, be sure to join in. There's nothing like getting grounded in the faith!

Come to Mary: 6633 County Road 13, Conejos, CO 81129. (719) 376-5985. ologp.com.

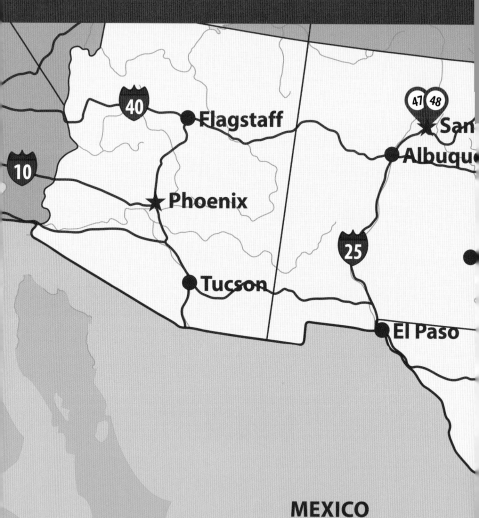

SOUTHWEST

Texas

45 ▸ WINDTHORST

Dedicate your church to the Blessed Mother and you're in good hands. Our Lady looked after **St. Mary's Catholic Church** in Windthorst — a small German dairy town twenty-five miles south of Wichita Falls — so well that she got her own highway and two grottoes. The first grotto inspired the second, the "grotto of gratitude."

When parishioner Charles Lindeman lost his wife, Mary, on January 10, 1941, he was distraught with grief. Mary left behind thirteen children at home, the youngest just three months old. (A fourteenth child was a sister at a Benedictine monastery in Arkansas.) The widower spent much time in prayer at St. Mary's Church, asking heaven for guidance and help.

One day, a kind soul gave the rectory housekeeper a statue of the Blessed Mother. "Would you like to make a shrine for the statue in memory of your wife?" the housekeeper asked Lindeman, hoping it would help heal his pain.

Lindeman and four of his sons began collecting rock to build a small grotto outside the Romanesque brick church, about 1925. When the hilltop grotto was finished, St. Mary's pastor, Fr. Francis Zimmerer, OSB, announced that he would bless it the following Sunday afternoon after Benediction. As fate had it, that Sunday was December 7, 1941 — the day Japan bombed Pearl Harbor. America was at war. Within days, the first Windthorst man left to fight, followed by dozens more.

The Windthorst women began flocking to the grotto and flooded Our Lady with tears and prayers. "Bring our husbands, sons, fathers, brothers, and boyfriends back home safely," they pleaded. Every Tuesday evening, after the cows had been milked, parishioners gathered in the church — like a battalion of soldiers — to storm heaven with novenas to Our Lady of Perpetual Help (see Boston, Massachusetts, site 4).

"Mother of Perpetual Help, we call upon your most powerful name," they prayed in one accord. "Your very name inspires confidence and hope."

In 1942, before leaving for combat, two parish men inspired Father Zimmerer and the congregation to enter into a spiritual contract with the Blessed Mother. They vowed to build a larger grotto in honor of Our Lady of Perpetual Help if every Windthorst soldier came home alive. As a sign of their vow, the soldiers began sending home a portion of their military pay to fund the grotto.

Then Father Zimmerer joined the "Windthorst boys": He enlisted as an army chaplain and served in the South Pacific until war's end in 1945. In all, sixty-four men — roughly twenty percent of the rural community's population — went off to war.

Month after month, year after year, the novenas continued at St. Mary's. When weeks passed with no letters from the warfront, the distraught women ran to the Blessed Mother for consolation and prayed even more prayers.

Miraculously, every soldier came home alive. All sixty-four of them!

Construction of the promised grotto — a larger version of the first grotto with a statue of the Immaculate Conception — began in 1949. Overseeing its design and construction was Fr. Patrick O'Neill, OSB, of St. Bernard's Abbey in Cullman, Alabama, famous for its Ave Maria Grotto and miniature grottos of sacred sites. The Windthorst men, who had

fought on land, air, sea, and under the sea, hauled in truckloads of native stone as well as granite from the Wichita Mountains in Oklahoma. St. Mary's Grotto was dedicated on August 22, 1950. All sixty-four veterans were in attendance, a living testimony to Our Lady's intercession.

Nestled in a hill below St. Mary's Church, the cross-topped cave measures about thirty feet wide by twenty feet tall. Above the granite altar stands a five-foot Italian marble statue of Our Lady of Perpetual Help. Mock stalactites cling to the ceiling, the walls decorated with colored glass, stones, and marbles. A needlepoint banner of sixty-four stars tells another story: The fifty-eight blue stars represent the soldiers who returned with no wounds; the eight silver stars, their comrades injured at war.

A bronze plaque proclaims, "In gratitude to Our Lady of Perpetual Help who returned us without a single fatality from World War II." Another plaque reads, "Their prayers were answered."

Located on US Highway 281 — a cross-country highway extending from the Canada–North Dakota border and running 1,875 miles south to the Texas–Mexico border — the grotto is dubbed "Our Lady of Highway 281." Truck drivers stop to ask Mary's protection on the heavily traveled road; other travelers light votive candles or write prayer intentions in a notebook. All find comfort in this roadside oasis of peace.

Come to Mary: 101 Church Street, Windthorst, TX 76389. (940) 423-6687. stmarysstboniface.com.

"Our Lady of Highway 281" — St. Mary's Grotto, St. Mary's Catholic Church, Windthorst, Texas

Signs and Wonders

When the Windthorst soldiers returned from World War II, many told incredible tales of survival, as though an invisible hand or a supernatural force had diverted bullets and grenades away from them. Their stories were later recounted in North Texas newspapers.

Oscar Gehring, who fought the Axis Powers in Europe, was spotted by a Nazi surveillance plane that let fly a hailstorm of bullets. Amazingly, every bullet kissed the dirt around his feet. Louis Lindemann survived the D-Day assault on the beaches of Normandy and the long march across France into Germany.

On the Pacific front, Clarence Wolf, who always carried a rosary with him, lived to tell about the invasion of Okinawa, taken yard by bloody yard. On the Island of Guam, John Hoff was the sole survivor of his platoon, all killed one terrible day by a Japanese hand grenade.

But A. R. Lindeman's harrowing tale on Okinawa was more than "lady luck," reported Bernadette Pruitt of *The Dallas Morning News*. One day, Lindeman and a California soldier were crouched in a foxhole when a mortar shell exploded, shredding the butt of Lindeman's rifle. Warm fluid began running down Lindeman's back.

"I believe I've been hit," he told his foxhole mate.

Lindeman turned to look at his comrade and froze. The blood wasn't his own. His mate had taken the fatal shell.

"Later, I took off my helmet and there were two holes in it, big enough to stick a finger through," Lindeman told Pruitt. "Shrapnel had gone in and out, somehow missing my head."

Were the Windthorst boys a miracle? Only heaven can say for sure, but something extraordinary happened in this small Texas town. Sixty-four men went off to war, and sixty-four men came home.

46 ▶ SAN JUAN

Can one miracle beget another? Visit the **Basilica of Our Lady of San Juan del Valle National Shrine**, just over the Mexico border, and you'll hear two miracle stories in one. Amazingly, the two events happened nearly 350 years apart — in two towns named San Juan.

In 1623, a family of traveling acrobats stopped in the Mexican town of San Juan de los Lagos, near Guadalajara, to give a performance. As the family was practicing their act, the youngest daughter fell to her death. But when a small statue of the Immaculate Conception was placed on her body, the dead girl sprang to life! Devotion to Mary, under the title of La Virgen de San Juan, spread across Mexico and later the American Southwest.

Fast forward to 1920, when Fr. Alfonso Jalbert, a member of the Oblates of Mary Immaculate, built a small wooden chapel in San Juan, Texas. In 1949, Fr. José María Azpiazu, OMI, the town's new pastor, commissioned a wooden replica of the Virgen de San Juan in Mexico. An *imagen de vestir* — a statue dressed in clothes — the Virgen is attired in exquisite robes fit for a queen. The chapel became a pilgrimage destination for both Mexican-Americans and Mexicans who couldn't make the long journey to pay homage to La Virgen de Guadalupe in Mexico City or La Virgen in San Juan de los Lagos.

To accommodate the growing throngs, a larger church was dedicated in 1954. The multitudes only increased. Farm migrant workers stopped here before following the harvest season north, asking for

Exterior mosaic — Basilica of Our Lady of San Juan del Valle National Shrine, San Juan, Texas

traveling mercies in their old cars and for bountiful work. On their way home, they stopped again to offer thanksgiving and to leave tokens of affection for the Virgen. The poor and the sick came to their heavenly Madre for solace and comfort.

"As weekly attendance jumped from thousands to tens of thousands," noted Father Azpiazu in *Handbook of Texas Online*, "the shrine was lavishly ornamented with oil paintings, wood carvings, stained-glass windows, and statues." The shrine grounds

expanded to include a pilgrim house, a cafeteria, a grade school, and a nursing home. The Virgen de San Juan became a mega attraction in South Texas.

On October 23, 1970, the unfathomable happened. While fifty priests were concelebrating Mass with another fifty worshippers in the pews, and 100 school children in an adjacent cafeteria, a deranged pilot deliberately crashed his small plane into the church. The church burst into flames, but miraculously no one inside was hurt.

"A steel beam prevented the plane from falling into the sanctuary," continued Father Azpiazu. "The pilot was the only fatality." Both the Blessed Sacrament and the Virgen image were rescued from the great ball of fire.

Heaven turned tragedy into triumph. In 1980, ten years after the plane catastrophe, today's Basilica of Our Lady of San Juan del Valle National Shrine was dedicated. Seating two thousand — more than twice the seating capacity of the old church — the 55,000-square-foot, contemporary limestone church is a jaw-dropper. Greeting pilgrims on the exterior, a massive Jesus mosaic presents his Mother, the Virgen de San Juan, to the Rio Grande Valley.

Step inside and your eyes are pulled to the Virgencita in the sanctuary, "set like a jewel at the center of a series of concentric circles," explained *Virgen de San Juan Shrine*, a bilingual booklet. "Mary's role as queen of heaven and earth is indicated by golden rays, as though emanating from a sun, with the traditional twelve stars."

Standing on the outer circle of this multistory artwork, sculpted by Spanish artisans in high-relief ceramic, are life-size figures of Mary's children who come here to pray: the sick, migrant families, a mother and her baby, the elderly, and religious sisters and clergy. The Virgen statue, about three feet tall, stands at the very center of the spectacular sculpture.

The curved sanctuary and nave replicate the shape of the quarter moon under the Virgen's feet.

Devotion to Mary continues in a great faceted-glass window, with symbols illustrating the Rosary mysteries. Some symbols compel reflection. What does the mountain road represent? Which mystery does the olive branch portray? Windows in the Candle Room portray the Presentation of the Lord. As prescribed by Jewish law, Mary presents the Christ Child and Joseph offers a pair of doves.

The shrine grounds include life-size bronze Stations of the Cross, set among palm trees, and a giant holy-water fountain that would put the most senior devils to flight.

The new, larger shrine drew even larger masses. Averaging more than one million pilgrims annually — or 20,000 per weekend — attendance rivals the great shrines of Europe. In Mexican-American tradition, Mariachi bands play at weekend Masses.

San Juan de los Lagos, Mexico, and San Juan, Texas: two famous Marian shrines with a miraculous Mother — La Virgen de San Juan.

Come to Mary: 400 North Virgen de San Juan Boulevard, San Juan, TX 78589. (956) 787-0033. olsjbasilica.org.

Signs and Wonders

When Fr. José María Azpiazu, OMI, was assigned to San Juan, Texas, in 1949, he commissioned an artist in Guadalajara, Mexico, to create a small wooden replica of the miracle statue of La Virgen de San Juan in San Juan de los Lagos, Mexico. When the statue was finished, the priest and two church members drove the 550 miles to Guadalajara to pick up the statue and to pay homage to the Virgen at her shrine in San Juan de los Lagos.

Around 425 miles into the journey, the driver lost control of the car near San Luis Potosi, Mexico, and the car slid down a mountainside. The threesome got out of the car, climbed back up to the road, and flagged down a truck driver who pulled the car back onto the road. The pilgrims continued to a nearby village, where they spent the night.

The next morning, they went back to the scene of the accident and gasped in amazement. Not only had the car suffered no damage, but "if they had gone off the road a few feet father along, they would have gone over a precipice and probably been killed," noted the booklet *Virgen de San Juan Shrine*.

It was then Father Azpiazu promised to build the Virgen a worthy shrine back home in San Juan. Dedicated in 1954, the shrine became a major pilgrimage destination in South Texas not only for Mexican-Americans but for Catholics in Mexico as well. The shrine would also bear witness to the world.

On October 23, 1970, a plane crashed into the shrine and exploded in flames. The full motive of the pilot, a former schoolteacher, was never discovered — but what was intended for evil only elevated Our Lady's status as a protective mother and patroness. The fifty priests inside — half the priests of the Diocese of Brownsville, it was said at the time — escaped the fireball. Even the skeptics called it a miracle.

La Virgen de San Juan de los Lagos

The legend of La Virgen de San Juan de los Lagos ("the Virgin of Saint John of the Lakes") is a "high-flying act." Around the turn of the seventeenth century, Spanish Franciscans brought a small image of the Immaculate Conception to the village church in San Juan de los Lagos, near Guadalajara in the Mexican province of Jalisco.

In 1623, a traveling acrobat family — a husband, his wife, and their two daughters — stopped in the village to give a performance. Much like trapeze artists today, the family's stunts included swinging on ropes high in the air. Adding more excitement, the artists flew "over swords and knives that were stuck in the ground with their points positioned upward," noted Joan Carroll Cruz in *Miraculous Images of Our Lady*.

One day, when the family was practicing their act, the youngest daughter, a mere child of six or seven years, fell on the knives and was killed. The grief-stricken family wrapped the dead girl in burial cloths and brought the body to the village church for burial. The caretaker at the church, an old Indian woman, begged the family to place the image of La Virgen on the girl and pray. As they did so, the shrouded corpse began to move! The girl had come back to life.

Made of cornstalks and glue, the Virgen statue had become brittle with age. In gratitude for his daughter's life, the father asked to take the image to Guadalajara and have it restored. As the acrobat made his way into Guadalajara, a man approached him and asked if he had a statue in need of repair. They agreed on a price, and the father gave him the icon. Some days later, the statue was returned "beautifully restored, with the face and hands of exceptional beauty," continued Cruz.

When the father went to thank the artist, he was nowhere to be found. Nobody knew a thing about him. Who was he? Some believe it was Saint Joseph, the faithful husband of the Blessed Virgin Mary, Our Lady of San Juan.

Centuries later, the Cathedral Basilica of San Juan de los Lagos is one of Mexico's most popular pilgrimage destinations, second only to the Basilica of Our Lady of Guadalupe in Mexico City.

Our Lady of San Juan's principal feasts are February 2, Candlemas Day, and December 8, feast of the Immaculate Conception.

New Mexico

SANTA FE

47

Santa Fe, New Mexico, is old. It boasts the country's oldest capital (1610), the oldest extant church (San Miguel Chapel, about 1610), the oldest community celebration, and the oldest Marian statue — **La Conquistadora** — who reigns from the country's oldest extant Marian shrine, a 1714 adobe side chapel in the Cathedral Basilica of St. Francis of Assisi.

Just how old is La Conquistadora? Nobody knows (a lady never reveals her age!), but she's at least four hundred years old. It's believed the twenty-eight-inch wooden statue was carved in Spain and carried by ship to Mexico. In early 1626, Franciscan priest Alonso de Benavides brought the polychrome icon to Santa Fe (Spanish for "Holy Faith") and enthroned her in the villa's adobe church, now the site of the cathedral basilica.

But a hole in the core of the statue has historians baffled. Who made the hole and why? Was the Lady mounted atop a staff and carried as a standard in the Crusades against the Moors? Or carried in religious processions back in her homeland? The mystery only adds to Our Lady's allure.

The title La Conquistadora, however, isn't about conquering in battle. Rather, Our Lady "conquers" (or wins) people through her love and that of her Son. And what stories her startling blue eyes tell: stories of a miraculous healing and a prophecy, a perpetual promise, and a wardrobe fit for a Spanish queen.

An *imagen de vestir* (a clothed statue), Our Lady's wardrobe would be the envy of any woman. Her walk-in closet is filled with handmade wigs (some fashioned from hair donated by cancer patients), bejeweled crowns and lace mantillas, rosaries galore, strings of pearls, earrings with gems of every kind, and hundreds of gowns donated by devotees.

One cape was made from vestments worn by Archbishop Jean Baptiste Lamy, the first American prelate of the Wild West immortalized in Willa Cather's 1927 classic *Death Comes for the Archbishop*. A Pueblo Indian artist created a Native American dress with tiny silver bracelets and a squash blossom necklace. Other gowns commemorate a priest's ordination day, while happy brides donate white dresses for Our Lady to wear on their wedding day.

It hasn't always been a peaceful reign for La Conquistadora on the rugged frontier of northern New Mexico, as Fray Angelico Chavez, a native New Mexican and Franciscan priest-historian-artist-poet, documented in *La Conquistadora: The Autobiography of an Ancient Statue*. One tumultuous event began with a warning.

In 1674, ten-year-old María Romero of Santa Fe, violently ill with fever (other accounts say she was crippled since childhood), was praying before a statue of Our Lady of the Blessed Sacrament of Toledo in her room. At that very moment, Our Lady cured the girl and told her, "Daughter, rise up and announce that the Custody [the Spanish colony] will soon be destroyed because of the lack of reverence it has for my priests, and that this miracle will be testimony of

La Conquistadora carried in her annual procession — Cathedral Basilica of St. Francis of Assisi, Santa Fe, New Mexico

the truth; and that the people must make amends for their guilt unless they wish to be punished further."

The girl arose and alerted the villa padre of Our Lady's prophetic visit. The Spaniards amended their ways, and good will began to flow once again between the Franciscan friars and their flocks.

Meanwhile, tension between the Pueblo Indians and the Spaniards continued to escalate. Like the Inquisition in Spain, Spanish colonial rule was often ruthless. Pueblo Indians were forced to pay tribute in corn and textiles, labor in Spanish fields, and convert to Catholicism. Pueblo *kivas* (underground ceremonial chambers) were destroyed, and traditional dances and other native rituals quashed.

On August 10, 1680, Our Lady's chastisement came to pass. Known as the Pueblo Revolt of 1680, many Pueblos banded together and attacked with a vengeance, torching churches and killing twenty-one friars and over 400 Spanish settlers. In Santa Fe, sacristan Josefa López Zambrano de Grijalva dashed into the burning church and rescued La Conquistadora from eternal doom. It's said the statue began to weep: Her children — Indian and Spanish — were maiming and killing each other.

Some two thousand Spaniards, along with hundreds of Pueblo Indians not aligned with the Revolt, and Our Lady fled three hundred miles south to the borderlands of present-day El Paso, Texas, and Cuidad Juárez, Mexico.

Twelve years later, in mid-September 1692, Diego de Vargas — the new governor of the exiled Spanish colony — and a contingent of soldiers, friars, and Indian auxiliaries rode into Santa Fe to reclaim the villa and the Kingdom of New Mexico for God and Spain. According to tradition, Governor de Vargas knelt at La Conquistadora's feet before the Entrada ("entry") and solemnly promised, "If a treaty is reached without bloodshed, an annual novena of Masses will be offered in your honor for perpetuity."

Armed with prayer, Governor de Vargas was also gracious: It's said that he served the Pueblo Indians hot chocolate, a drink that originated in Mexico. The Indians agreed to peace, and on September 14 — feast of the Exaltation of the Holy Cross — they erected a tall cross on the plaza near the extant Palace of the Governors. (The Spaniards' actual resettlement of Santa Fe in late 1693, however, wasn't without bloodshed.)

Governor de Vargas died in 1704 before he could fulfill his promise to Our Lady. In 1712, Lieutenant Governor Juan Páez Hurtado and other governing authorities made good his pledge and issued an official Pregón de la Fiesta ("Fiesta proclamation") mandating an annual event with "Vespers, Mass, Sermon, and Procession through the Main Plaza." And thus began the country's oldest community celebration in honor of the country's oldest Madonna.

More than three centuries later, Governor de Vargas's vow continues to be honored. On the Sunday following Corpus Christi Sunday, the annual Novena Masses of Thanksgiving in honor of La Conquistadora begin with a Pontifical High Mass at the cathedral basilica. That afternoon, a procession takes Our Lady from her cathedral chapel to Rosario Chapel at Rosario Cemetery, near the hillside site where legend holds Governor de Vargas once prayed.

But this isn't just any procession. The cathedral bells peal. The streets clear. Our Lady — attired in exquisite robes and jewels and carried high on a palanquin — is passing by! The following Sunday, Our Lady is returned in procession to the cathedral basilica.

Fiesta de Santa Fe — both a religious and a civic event — is held in late summer and opens with a Mass at Rosario Chapel and the reading of the Pregón by the city mayor. Religious observances include a candlelight procession to the hilltop Cross of the Martyrs, a memorial to the slain Franciscan friars, where prayers are offered for intercultural harmony and peace.

Civic events include parades, traditional New Mexican food, Indian and Spanish colonial crafts, and cheers of *¡Qué Viva La Fiesta!* Long live the Fiesta!

And so it goes, century after century. *¡Qué Viva La Conquistadora!* Long reign La Conquistadora, Our Lady of Peace!

For more about the history of the Catholic Church in New Mexico, "read" the cathedral basilica's great sculpted bronze doors. Twenty scenes depict key events, including the arrival of the first Spanish colonists in 1598 and La Conquistadora's escape from the Pueblo Revolt in 1680. In Old World tradition, the doors are tall enough for the archbishop (or pope) to enter on a horse.

Come to Mary: Cathedral Basilica of St. Francis of Assisi: 131 Cathedral Place, Santa Fe, NM 87501. (505) 982-5619. cbsfa.org; Fiesta de Santa Fe: santafefiesta.org.

Signs and Wonders

There's hardly a time during the day when La Conquistadora is alone in her adobe chapel at the Cathedral Basilica of St. Francis of Assisi. Anglos, Hispanics, and Indians all flock to her with petitions and prayers of thanksgiving. They bring flowers, light candles, and kneel before her throne on a Spanish colonial reredos with admiration and love. Even doubting tourists pay her a visit.

But on March 19, 1973, her procession of devotees came to a standstill. The centuries-old statue had been kidnapped! Grown men and women wept in the streets.

State and local police were summoned to investigate the theft. Was the abduction related to the theft of other religious art around town? In July 1972, a valuable statue of St. Michael the Archangel and other icons and paintings had been stolen from historic San Miguel Chapel.

"According to one theory, La Conquistadora had gone off in search of the lost San Miguel because he'd been gone so long and couldn't find his way back home!" wrote Richard Melzer, a New Mexico author and historian, in *La Crónica de Nuevo Mexico.*

Catholics across the region began plying their beads and did acts of penance for her swift and safe return. "La Conquistadora, come home," they prayed. "We love you!" The mayor of Santa Fe declared March 25 a day of mourning.

The case broke two weeks later on Saturday, April 7, when cathedral priest Fr. Miguel Baca received a ransom letter demanding $150,000 for the statue. Enclosed was a cross from La Conquistadora's crown.

The letter instructed Father Baca to ring the cathedral bells ten times at 4:45 p.m. on Wednesday, April 11. If the priest did as he was told, the kidnappers promised to deliver additional instructions by phone the next day. Father Baca rang the bells ten times at precisely 4:45 p.m., but the phone call didn't come as promised. It came two days later.

Police traced the call to a local minor, who confessed and implicated an accomplice, and then led police to an abandoned mine in the Manzano Mountains near Albuquerque. There, the police found La Conquistadora, snugly wrapped in foam padding. Also found were the sacred artifacts from San Miguel Chapel. (See, Our Lady really did go searching!)

Cathedral bells pealed as La Conquistadora rode triumphantly back into Santa Fe — to the police station where she spent time in custody as criminal evidence. "It's a *milagro*," everyone said. "A miracle!" Maybe a bigger miracle than they thought. A large quantity of explosives was later discovered in the mine, "making La Conquistadora's survival in the mine even more miraculous," continued Melzer.

Back on her throne, La Conquistadora is again conquering hearts with her love and that of her Son. It's been Our Lady's way for four centuries and hopefully for many more centuries to come.

La Conquistadora

La Conquistadora is a statue of many titles. When she arrived in Santa Fe in 1626, she was enshrined in the villa's adobe church as Our Lady of the Assumption. When a more sumptuous adobe church was built about 1630 and dedicated to the Immaculate Conception, her title changed too. Along the way, she was also called Our Lady of the Rosary.

Locally, Our Lady is popularly called La Conquistadora. "For throughout all Spanish America, the first image of Mary that came to a pioneer city was given this title," explained Fray Angelico Chavez in the booklet *The Santa Fe Cathedral.* One definition of the Spanish verb *conquistar* is to "win the heart of."

In 1992, acknowledging the injustices inflicted by the Spanish colonists upon the Pueblo Indians, and pledging to preserve their indigenous culture and native traditions, Archbishop Robert F. Sánchez of Santa Fe bestowed yet another title upon La Conquistadora: Our Lady of Peace.

SANTA FE

Where is America's oldest extant shrine to Our Lady of Guadalupe? In Santa Fe, our nation's oldest capital, of course! The **Santuario de Guadalupe** and Our Lady's escapades defy earthly odds, but is anything too difficult for the Celestial Lady and her Son? She left her miraculous image on Juan Diego's tilma to convince the bishop to build a church on Tepeyac Hill in Mexico City, and she worked miracles to keep her shrine on a hill in Santa Fe.

The Santa Fe saga begins about 1777, when Franciscan friars built the adobe sanctuary as a pilgrims' shrine. As mud churches went, the shrine had a flat roof, a packed dirt floor, no pews, a ladder to access the choir loft, and an enormous 1783 oil canvas painting of Nuestra Señora de Guadalupe and her apparitions to St. Juan Diego. According to traditions at the time, Mexican artist José de Alzibar painted the Virgen with a multi-pointed crown (see Conejos, Colorado, site 44.)

The sixteen-by-twenty-foot painting was cut in strips, hauled by burro pack-trains up the Camino Real — the 1,500-mile Royal Road from Mexico City via Chihuahua to Santa Fe — and sewn back together in Santa Fe. (Look closely, and you'll detect stitches.) Amazingly, Our Lady's painting survived the six-month journey.

In 1826, the adobe was crumbling and called unfit for worship. Nevertheless, the sanctuary survived, and in 1881, it became the parish church for English-speaking settlers. Fr. James H. Defouri, the first pastor and a French native, "baptized" the adobe with a New England look: a pitched roof with a tall steeple (painted a bright orange!), mock-Gothic windows, and pews. He also enclosed the churchyard with a white picket fence.

"He complained bitterly that people and dogs made a shortcut across church property and made a practice of cutting his flowers," reported the *Santa Fean* magazine. "Not only this, but worst of all he had observed somebody walking a pig on a string straight through his gardens."

A fire in 1922 took the New England steeple and much of the roof, and ruined the frescoes inside. Providentially, the thick adobe walls and the Virgen's altarpiece escaped harm. The church was repaired and born again — this time to the California Mission style. In the 1960s, the adobe was closed and fell into disrepair.

The Virgen didn't want to leave Santa Fe. She had faith in her Spanish colonial descendants and began speaking to their hearts, "Save the shrine! Save the shrine!" In the 1970s, the two-hundred-year-old sanctuary was restored and retrofitted (mostly) to its original Spanish colonial design. The shrine became a cultural attraction, and Our Lady of Guadalupe — the Star of the New Evangelization and the Patroness of the Americas — witnessed to throngs of tourists.

Our Lady's fame grew in 2002, when a local museum exhibited sacrilegious images of Guadalupana. In reparation for the blasphemies, Santa Fe devotees decided to fight evil with good and make Mary's piety known to even more people. They commissioned Mexico City artist Georgina Farias to sculpt a twelve-foot bronze statue of La Virgen de Guadalupe for the sanctuary grounds.

The Virgen's travels to Santa Fe captivated the nation. On July 13, 2008, accompanied by a group of Santa Fe pilgrims, the strikingly beautiful statue began her journey from Mexico City up the Cami-

no Real — the same historic route that brought the first Spanish colonists here in 1598. When the dark-skinned Virgen reached the border, the unthinkable happened: The United States Border Patrol took the statue into custody and X-rayed her like a common criminal for contraband. No drugs were found.

Then, the Virgen went missing. Nobody knew where the 4,000-pound statue was! People everywhere were glued to their radio and television sets.

Rather than praying to the Virgen, people began praying *for* the Virgen. The bubble-wrapped icon was found a couple of days later in an El Paso, Texas, warehouse. Her "immigrant" papers had gotten lost.

The Virgen returned the prayer-favor of her people. During the dedication ceremony on August 15, the feast of her Assumption into heaven, a cloud-burst drenched the pilgrims on Santa Fe's Tepeyac Hill. But when the statue was unveiled, rays of brilliant sunshine pieced the dark sky. Our Lady seemed to be saying — just as she did to Juan Diego in 1531 — "Am I not here, who is your Mother?"

Come to Mary: Agua Fria and Guadalupe Streets, Santa Fe, NM 87501. (505) 983-8868. santuariodeguadalupesantafe.com.

La Virgen de Guadalupe, Georgina Farias — Santuario de Guadalupe, Santa Fe, New Mexico

Signs and Wonders

What are the odds?

That an enormous oil painting of Our Lady of Guadalupe's apparitions to Juan Diego, carried by burros from Mexico City, Mexico, to Santa Fe, New Mexico — a distance of 1,500 miles — arrived on the Spanish colonial frontier unharmed?

That Our Lady's adobe church, once called unfit for worship, still stands?

That Our Lady's oil painting escaped serious damage in a fire that destroyed the church frescoes?

That Our Lady's twelve-foot statue went lost and found?

That the statue stands at the end of the Camino de Real, the same historic road that brought the first Spanish colonists and Our Lady's piety to Santa Fe and northern New Mexico in 1598 — just sixty-seven years after she appeared to Juan Diego in 1531?

That rays of light pierced stormy clouds during the statue's dedication ceremony in 2008?

That tourists of every belief (and no belief) visit the Santuario and pray at her outdoor statue?

What are the odds?

Our Lady's odds!

Our Lady of Guadalupe

On Saturday, December 9, 1531, Juan Diego, a widower and an Aztec Indian convert, was on his way to what is now Mexico City to attend Mass in honor of Our Lady. He was walking by a hill called Tepeyac, when he heard the heavenly music of songbirds. Suddenly, a young lady dressed like an Aztec maiden appeared before him, her clothes shining like the sun.

"I am the Holy Virgin Mary, Mother of God," the dark-skinned Lady said. "Go to the Franciscan Bishop Juan de Zumarraga and tell him I desire a chapel to be built here."

The bishop listened to Juan Diego's fanciful story and sent him on his way. Juan Diego returned to Tepeyac Hill and told the Lady what happened.

"Go see the bishop again and make known my wish for a chapel," she told him.

Juan Diego went the following day, Sunday, to the bishop's palace and repeated the Lady's request.

"Ask the Lady for a sign," the bishop replied, dismissing Juan Diego a second time.

Juan Diego returned to Tepeyac Hill and told the Virgen about the bishop's demand.

"Come here tomorrow for the sign," she replied.

But Juan Diego's uncle had fallen gravely ill and, rather than meeting Our Lady as planned, he went to find a doctor. That night the uncle begged Juan Diego to summon a priest to give him the last rites.

Early the next morning, Juan Diego set out to find a priest, sheepishly avoiding the apparition site and the Lady. But the Lady found Juan Diego and assured him that his uncle would live. Heeding the bishop's request for a sign, she instructed Juan Diego to climb a hill and pick the roses he would find there. When Juan Diego reached the hilltop, he blinked his eyes in wonder. Before him was a bed of Castilian roses — roses in December, in the dead of winter!

When Juan Diego returned with the roses, the Lady arranged them in his tilma. Once again, he trekked to the bishop's palace. When Juan Diego opened the tilma before the bishop, the prelate fell to his knees. On the tilma was an image of the Virgen, just as she had appeared on Tepeyac Hill!

The date was December 12, celebrated today as the feast of Our Lady of Guadalupe.

Bishop Zumarraga erected a chapel on Tepeyac Hill, which evolved into the Basilica of Our Lady of Guadalupe, where the miraculous tilma is still venerated today.

The dark-skinned Virgen is typically portrayed as "a woman clothed with the sun, with the moon under her feet" (Rv 12:1). Her eyes are downcast, her hands folded in prayer. It's said the stars on the Virgen's turquoise mantle mimic the stars in the December sky at the time of her visits to Juan Diego.

PACIFIC WEST

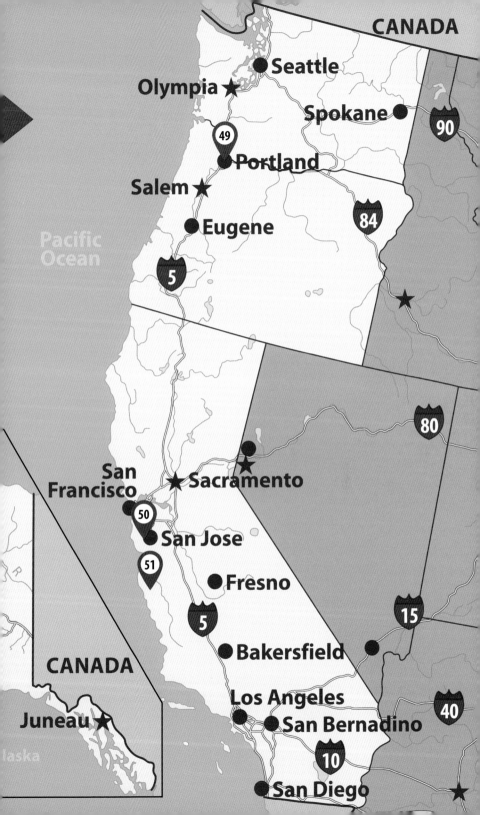

Oregon

49 ▶ PORTLAND

How powerful are the prayers of a nine-year-old boy? Powerful enough to bend the Blessed Mother's ears and build the renowned **National Sanctuary of Our Sorrowful Mother** (popularly called The Grotto) in Portland. The Grotto is also a love story — a boy's love for two mothers, his mother on earth and Mother Mary in heaven above.

The story unfolds in 1892, when little Peter Mayer learned his mother lay dying after giving birth to a baby girl. With hot tears trailing down his cheeks, the Canadian lad ran to St. Mary's Church in Kitchener, Ontario, and entreated the Blessed Mother to save his mother's life. In return, Peter promised to one day do a "great work for the Church."

Both mother and baby sister lived.

Little Peter grew up, answered heaven's call, and became a priest with the Order of Friar Servants of Mary (the Servites) — a mendicant order founded in 1240 by Our Lady herself — and took the name Ambrose. In 1918, Fr. Ambrose Mayer was assigned as the first Servite pastor in the Archdiocese of Portland, Oregon.

His boyhood vow ever on his mind, the friar began looking for land in Portland. In 1923, he discovered a stretch of wild forest owned by the Union Pacific Railroad. Once used to quarry rock for rail beds, the parcel was slated to be sold as residential property. In Father Mayer's eyes, the untamed wilderness was a perfect site for a "natural cathedral" for the Queen of Heaven.

The price: $48,000, no small sum in the day. Father Mayer stuck his neck out in faith and bid $3,000 — every penny he had — as a down payment. He (and the Blessed Mother) got the property; a national campaign raised the balance. What happened next is truly spectacular. A massive cave-grotto was carved out of the base of a 110-foot-tall basalt cliff.

Measuring approximately thirty feet wide, thirty feet deep, and nearly fifty feet high, Our Lady's Grotto has changed little over the years. Commanding the viewer's attention, a Pietà replica — carved of Carrera marble like Michelangelo's masterpiece — rests atop a stone pillar, flanked by the original bronze angels bearing lighted torches. The stone altar, communion rail, pedestals, and pulpit are original as well. The stunningly beautiful sanctuary was dedicated on May 29, 1924, the words of the dedication prayer still relevant today.

"Let this be a sanctuary of peace for all peoples of the earth and surely in this day a sanctuary is needed," invoked Archbishop Alexander Christie of Portland. "Torn with differences, strife, and grief, the world needs sanctuary where the human spirit can seek peace and consolation."

As little Peter promised Our Lady, The Grotto is indeed "a great work." Built on two levels and encompassing sixty-two acres of meandering forested and flower-lined paths, The Grotto honors the Blessed Mother in many settings and statues.

Located on the plaza level is Our Lady's Grotto. The plaza level also holds the Christus Statue (1931), an immense German-cast bronze sculpture of Jesus carrying the cross. His right hand points to a lofty bronze statue of Our Sorrowful Mother (1933) standing atop the cliff — 150 feet directly above the Grotto — as though saying, "Behold your mother!" (Jn 19:27). The Chapel of Mary, Mother of the Human Race (1955) touts a 110-foot bell tower with a mosaic of Mother and Child.

On the upper level (a ten-story elevator connects the two levels) are found the Via Matris (1930), the Way of Our Sorrowful Mother with seven stations that portray sorrowful events in her life, and winding walkways dotted with wayside shrines. Ethnic shrines include Our Lady of Czestochowa (Poland), Our Lady of Guadalupe (Mexico), and Our Lady of La Vang (Vietnam). A Filipino shrine, the Dambana (Tagalog for "altar") is shaped like a *salakot*, the traditional head gear of Filipino women.

The little red St. Anne's Chapel (1934), built to house the Blessed Sacrament during the country's first Marian Congress, honors Mary's earthly mother, Saint Anne, and displays Madonna paintings from many countries. On a clear day, you can see forever from the glass-walled Meditation Chapel (1991).

Take time to enjoy the Rose Garden (the rose is an ancient symbol of Mary) and the Peace Garden, the landscaping ingeniously using light and darkness to tell the Redemption story. Twenty bronze plaques depict the Mysteries of the Rosary.

The Grotto is famous for its Outdoor Mother's Day Mass (the first Mass in 1930 attracted over 30,000 pilgrims!) and the Christmas Festival of Lights, a Portland tradition since 1988.

Does Our Lady hear the prayers of nine-year-old boys? Visit The Grotto and you'll give a resounding yes!

Come to Mary: NE Eighty-Fifth Avenue and Sandy Boulevard, Portland, OR 97220. (503) 254-7371. thegrotto.org.

Signs and Wonders

More than 650 years before little Peter Mayer begged Our Lady to save his dying mother, the Seven Holy Founders of the Order of Friar Servants of Mary (the Servite Order) were having their own Marian encounters. According to Servite history, on August 15, 1233, the feast of the Assumption of the Blessed Virgin Mary, the seven men were deep in prayer when Our Lady appeared to them. Retreat from the world and live for God alone, she told them.

The men — prosperous cloth merchants in Florence, Italy — left behind their families and businesses and took refuge in a house outside the gates of Florence. When flocks of curious souls began seeking them out, the Seven Holy Founders took to the slopes of Monte Senario, where they built a hermitage.

On Good Friday 1240, legend holds, Our Lady appeared again to the seven men, bearing in her arms a black habit, while an angel held a scroll inscribed with the words "Servants of Mary." Our Lady asked them to found a religious order called the Servants of Mary, wear the black habit in memory of her Seven Sorrows, and follow the mendicant Rule of Saint Augustine. And thus the Order of Friar Servants of Mary was born.

The Servite Order today also includes women religious and lay men and women.

The Servites (servite.org) are known for the Rosary of the Seven Sorrows, the Black Scapular, and the Sorrowful Mother Novena, which began in 1937 at the Servites' Our Lady of Sorrows Basilica (ols-chicago.com) in Chicago, Illinois.

During World War II and into the 1950s, tens of thousands of devotees attended one of dozens of weekly services at the Italian Renaissance church, nicknamed the Joy of Chicago.

Our Lady of Sorrows

The devotion to Our Lady of Sorrows is rooted in Scripture. The Seven Sorrows of Mary (not to be confused with the Sorrowful Mysteries of the Rosary) are: the prophecy of Simeon (see Lk 2:25–35); the flight into Egypt (Mt 2:13–15); the loss of the Child Jesus in the Temple for three days (Lk 2:41–50); Mary meets Jesus on his way to Calvary (Lk 23:27–31; Jn 19:17); the Crucifixion and Death of Jesus (Jn 19:25–30); Jesus is taken down from the Cross (Lk 23:50–53; Jn 19:31–37); and the burial of Jesus (Mk 15:40–47; Lk 23:50–56; Jn 19:38–42).

In religious art, the Sorrowful Mother is often portrayed with either one or seven swords or daggers piercing her heart. The feast of Our Lady of Sorrows is aptly observed on September 15, the day after the feast of the Exaltation of the Holy Cross.

Califoria

SANTA CLARA

Our Lady of Peace Church and Shrine in Santa Clara is a miracle — miracle upon miracle upon miracle! Where else does a thirty-two-foot stainless steel statue of Mary literally stop traffic? And no wonder, the statue has a sure foundation — millions of Rosaries.

Our Lady's odyssey begins about 1960, when an explosion in population and housing growth was predicted for Santa Clara County, then a mostly rural area. To prepare for the flocks of new parishioners, the Archdiocese of San Francisco bought various properties, including thirteen acres of farmland for $130,000 in a Santa Clara real estate division marketed as New Bethlehem. In 1961, Fr. Joseph G. Sullivan was appointed founding pastor of Our Lady of Peace Church.

The church property, located in a pear orchard with dirt roads, was "out in the boondocks," as Father

Sullivan liked to say. The House of the Lord went up and was dedicated in 1963. That same year, the City of Santa Clara "voted to rezone most of the land within the parish boundaries for industrial development," reported Rosemary Alva in *Our Lady's Way*, a compilation of memories by clergy and parishioners.

Instead of new homes, office buildings would spring forth. Where would the people — and the money needed to pay off $500,000 in church debt — come from? The parish was small and poor, with immigrant fishermen, boat builders, and laborers and their families constituting the church rolls. The Sunday collection was often $30.

Fear not — this was New Bethlehem, after all! (*Bethlehem* is Hebrew for "House of Bread.") In 1969, Fr. John J. Sweeny, of Irish and Italian ancestry, arrived as pastor. "The women would say he looked like Dean Martin and sang like Bing Crosby," reminisced Deacon Daniel Hernandez in *Our Lady's Way*. But his heart belonged to Mary.

Father Sweeny, forty-five years old, surveyed his new parish. "I didn't have anything but a prayer," he later remarked. The priest initiated praying the Rosary before Mass and made confession available during Mass — in an era when these spiritual practices were falling by the wayside in many churches. He began perpetual adoration long before it became widely popular and established First Friday all-night vigils. In 1972, Father Sweeny and future priest Michael Pintacura launched the first Pilgrimage to Fátima Mass and Procession at Our Lady of Peace Church. As the pilgrimages grew, so did the number of healings reported.

Miracle! Church attendance boomed.

Meanwhile, the surrounding landscape changed

from pear orchards to high-tech office buildings, and Santa Clara Valley became known as Silicon Valley. While scoffers saw little hope for a church in a high-tech setting, Father Sweeny saw divine opportunity: A mega-statue of Mary near a freeway exit was evangelism at its best!

He presented his plans for a grand shrine to the Immaculate Heart of Mary to Archbishop Joseph T. McGucken of the Archdiocese of San Francisco (Santa Clara is now part of the Diocese of San Jose). The archbishop gave his consent but forbade any fundraising; the parish was already saddled with debt. That didn't stop Father Sweeny.

"Can I ask people to donate prayers?" he asked, entrusting the shrine to Mary.

"Of course," the archbishop replied.

Father Sweeny outlined his statuesque dream to his flock and asked for one million Rosaries as a prayer foundation for the shrine. Pray, and Our Lady will do the rest, he told them. To track the number of Rosaries prayed, Father Sweeny issued "rosary checks" — made payable to Our Lady — for people to record their Rosaries. As rosary checks began rolling in at the church, so did real checks for money.

Miracle! Father Sweeney got not one million but three million Rosaries!

Before long, parishioners and city folks alike knew Father Sweeney had an "in" with the Blessed Mother. He wanted the land in front of the church, near US Highway 101, for the outdoor shrine. When the land went up for auction and word got out that Father Sweeny was going to bid, other bidders backed off. Awesome Mary did it again — he got the property.

It took prayer and heaven, however, to find a

sculptor. The first sculptor contacted died a few months later. A second sculptor also passed away. In 1976, Father Sweeny found renowned artist Charles C. Parks of Wilmington, Delaware, exhibiting his works at a San Francisco art show. When the sculptor saw the proposed shrine site — a piece of property bordering two busy highways — he was appalled. Within eyesight was Marriott's Great America, an amusement park (now California's Great America), with a Ferris wheel!

A Ferris wheel with a view of the Blessed Mother? That didn't faze Father Sweeny. With every ascent of the Ferris wheel, riders would encounter Mother Mary, a spiritual high of sorts. Parks, a non-Catholic, couldn't turn Father Sweeney down. He was "as close to a saint as a man can be," Parks claimed in *Our Lady's Way*.

In the fall of 1977, Father Sweeny and the sculptor traveled to Fátima, Portugal, for artistic inspiration and to attend the sixtieth anniversary celebration of the Miracle of Fátima on October 13. They also consulted with an artist-cousin of Lúcia dos Santos — the oldest of the three shepherd children to whom Our Lady of Fátima appeared — to learn how she had described Our Lady. According to the cousin, Lúcia portrayed Our Lady as young, very beautiful, and full of light.

Back home in Delaware, Parks began working on the mega-Madonna, a stainless steel wonder. Our Lady's face is young and beautiful, with long tresses falling down her shoulders. Her dress — strips of welded stainless steel — is pure genius: Light reflect-

"The Awesome Madonna" — Our Lady of Peace Church and Shrine, Santa Clara, California

ing off the metal strips gives Mary an ethereal glow, even creating an aura about her. Our Lady's gown reveals her as an expectant mother.

Finally, after years of planning and creating, it was time to transport the nearly four-ton monument via flatbed truck to Santa Clara. Everywhere she stopped, people came out in droves to pay homage to the Lady. Meanwhile, a twelve-foot-tall landscaped mound was being prepared at Our Lady of Peace Church for the ginormous statue. The mound and statue together are taller than many four-story buildings.

On October 7, 1983, the feast of Our Lady of the Rosary, the Shrine to the Immaculate Heart of Mary — popularly called Our Lady of Peace Shrine — was dedicated. Participating in the three-day event was the Rosary Priest, Ven. Patrick Peyton, CSC, founder of the Family Rosary Crusade.

Cost of the statue: $340,000 in unsolicited donations. Miracle! Father Sweeny never asked for a dime — only prayers.

And so it happened that Our Lady, dubbed the Awesome Madonna, reigns over New Bethlehem and Silicon Valley. Hundreds of thousands of commuters pass by her daily, Mary's outstretched hands inviting them to stop for a moment of prayer and a spiritual hug. Many who do stop — Buddhist, Protestant, or Catholic — fall to their knees at her feet. Many weep in her presence; some slip written prayers into the folds of her metallic gown.

To this day, Our Lady of Peace Shrine is the only major Marian shrine on the West Coast between the National Sanctuary of Our Sorrowful Mother, commonly known as The Grotto (see site 49), in Portland, Oregon, nearly 700 miles to the north, and the

Basilica of Our Lady of Guadalupe in Mexico City, Mexico, over 2,100 miles to the south.

Our Lady of Peace Church and Shrine are open for around-the-clock prayer. Unless Mass is being offered, the Rosary is recited every hour on the hour. From May through October, on the thirteenth day of each month, the Fátima Pilgrimage Mass and Procession replicate the candlelight processions and blessings of the sick in Fátima, Portugal.

Come to Mary: 2800 Mission College Boulevard, Santa Clara, CA 95054. (408) 988-4585. olop-shrine.org.

Signs and Wonders

The monumental saga of Our Lady of Peace in Santa Clara, California, could have ended here, but it only grew and grew. When other Mary devotees saw the mega statue, they wanted one, too. Colossal statues of Mary sprang up in New Castle, Delaware (see site 9), St. John, Indiana (see site 23), and Sioux City, Iowa (see site 31), all with miracle stories of their own.

The Immaculate Heart of Mary

Devotion to the Immaculate Heart of Mary transcends the ages, but the piety ascended to new heights after Our Lady of Fátima's apparitions in 1917 to shepherd children Lúcia dos Santos and Francisco and Jacinta Marto (see Arapahoe, Nebraska, site 36). During her July 13 visit, Our Lady told the children, "God wishes to establish devotion to my Immaculate Heart to save souls from hell and bring about world peace."

In traditional iconography, the Immaculate Heart of Mary is often depicted with a sword piercing her heart, referencing Simeon's prophecy in Luke 2:35: "A sword will pierce through your own soul." In some artistic renditions, a band of white roses encircles Mary's heart, symbolizing both her Immaculate Conception and her pure heart.

The feast of the Immaculate of Heart of Mary is celebrated on the third Saturday after Pentecost.

CARMEL

51

She stands five-feet-two-inches tall and traveled with a five-foot-two-inch man. She wore a gown of rich brocade; he, a coarse bluish-gray robe. She was destined to become the "First Lady of California"; he, a saint. Who are they? Saint Junípero Serra and Nuestra Señora de Belén (Our Lady of Bethlehem). Their mystically entwined journey began in Mexico about 1768.

When rumors reached King Carlos III of Spain that Russia was planning to occupy Monterey Bay — the northernmost point of a five-hundred-mile stretch of coastal lands claimed by Spain as early as 1542 but never colonized — he moved a knight into position. He ordered José de Gálvez, Inspector General of New Spain, to secure the territory for God and Crown.

Gálvez enlisted Franciscan friar Junípero Serra, a Mallorca native, and together they laid out plans for the Sacred Expedition. Gálvez would establish garrisons at San Diego and Monterey, and Padre Serra would create a "ladder" of missions up the coastline of California, one every fifty miles, or a day's journey apart, to convert the natives.

Gálvez, a pious sort, also solicited divine help. He entrusted to Padre Serra a life-size wood statue of **Our Lady of Bethlehem**. Possibly carved in Spain, California's oldest statue looks human: She has brown glass eyes with real eyelashes and rosy cheeks. And like a human mother, she holds the Infant Jesus in the crook of her arm. Gálvez also made Padre Serra promise to return the Madonna once the cross was firmly planted in Monterey.

From her very first day in Alta California (the present-day State of California), Our Lady of Bethlehem had a dual role and title. In the Old World, Spanish and Portuguese sailors invoked her protection at sea. Here, in the New World, Our Lady not only performed nautical miracles but also duties as La Conquistadora, or Our Lady of Conquering Love. When Spanish Franciscans founded their New World missions, they looked to La Conquistadora for help in "conquering hearts" and leading souls to Christ. (See Cathedral Basilica of Santa Fe, site 48).

On March 28, 1769, Padre Serra, fifty-five years old and plagued with leg ulcers, began his 750-mile overland journey by mule up Baja California, Mexico, to San Diego in Alta California. Meanwhile, three ships were sailing north from Mexico. Aboard the San Antonio was Our Lady of Bethlehem. When Padre Serra arrived at San Diego Bay three months later, the news was grim.

The San Jose was lost at sea, and the "San Carlos had limped into San Diego Harbor, practically a ghost ship," wrote Gregory Orfalea in Journey to the Sun. "At least twenty-one of its sailors, and several of its twenty-five soldiers, had died at sea" of scurvy. Only the San Antonio, carrying Our Lady's statue, had arrived intact and with a full crew.

Did Saint Anthony, the wonderworker invoked in matters "lost and found," help the San Antonio find its way to California? Or did Our Lady of Bethlehem, patroness of mariners, protect the San Antonio from getting lost at sea? A question for eternity.

Padre Serra founded Mission San Diego Alcalá, the first of California's chain of twenty-one missions, on July 16, 1769, the feast of Our Lady of Mount

Carmel. After planting the traditional great cross on a hillock, he offered Mass under a canopy of branches, graced by Mary's statue. The Indian women must have thought the icon, with her penetrating glass eyes and red lips, was real: They brought food to fatten Mary up! Some women even tried to suckle the Infant.

Our Lady reigned over San Diego for nine months, until Padre Serra set his sights on evangelizing Monterey. On April 16, 1770, the San Antonio left the San Diego harbor; on board were Padre Serra and Our Lady. The Presidio-Mission San Carlos Borromeo was founded on June 3, 1770.

Padre Junípero Serra bid farewell to his Lady and sent her back to Inspector General Gálvez in Mexico City. The parting was surely sweet sorrow: Padre Serra and Our Lady, of the same height, gazing at each other, eyeball to glass eyeball.

Back in Mexico, the First Lady of California — who had sailed the Atlantic Ocean from the Iberian Peninsula to Mexico, the Pacific Ocean to San Diego and later to Monterey, then back to Mexico — was about to ride the seas again. Gálvez sent her back to Monterey. She was here to stay.

In 1771, Padre Serra separated the Monterey presidio and mission, and moved the mission five miles inland to Carmel. A "truly delightful spot," he described the site, overlooking the bay.

Our Lady served her people well on land and at sea. In letters dated May 1774, October 1775, and July 1779, Padre Serra made mention of offering special Masses to Our Lady to fulfill vows made by ship captains and sailors caught in tempests at sea. She also witnessed over 4,000 baptisms at Mission Carmel alone.

The 1,000th baptism was sprinkled with levity. According to lore, when Padre Serra baptized the adult Indian convert, he named him Millán Deogracias. Millán for San Millán de Cogolla (St. Emilian Cucullatus, a sixth-century Spanish saint), and because Millán is similar to *millar*, the Spanish word for one thousand. When combined with Deogracias, for Saint Deogratias whose Latin name means "Thanks be to God," the convert became "A thousand thanks to God!"

Padre Serra died August 28, 1784, at age seventy, and was buried in the mission chapel, known today as **Carmel Mission Basilica**. Our Lady of Bethlehem was with him in the beginning and she was there at the end. And she's still here today, conquering hearts for the love of God.

Come to Mary: 3080 Rio Road, Carmel, CA 93923. (831) 624-1271. carmelmission.org.

Signs and Wonders

Miracles wrought by Our Lady of Bethlehem at Mission Carmel didn't end with Padre Serra's death: One spectacular ex-voto is a foot-high silver crown. Translated, the Spanish inscription reads, "From the devotion of Naval Lieutenant Don Juan Bautista de Matute, Commander of the frigate *Purísima Concepción.* He dedicates this crown in fulfillment of a vow, year 1798."

• • • • •

After Mexico won its independence from Spain in 1821, the California mission period of evangelization waned. By 1834, Mission Carmel was secularized and the padres and the Indians forced off the land. Ranchers began grazing the land, and the mission fell into ruin. Another adventure awaited Our Lady.

According to Martin J. Morgado in *Junípero Serra's Legacy,* the Cantua family, one of the mission's last resident Indian families, swooped up Our Lady of Bethlehem and took her with them. Somehow, Our Lady became separated from her Infant and her crown. The Baby Jesus statue and crown would find their way to the Royal Presidio Chapel at Monterey.

When María Ignacia Dutra, a Cantua daughter, moved to Monterey in 1876, she took Our Lady with her and enshrined the statue in her home. Many devotees came to pay homage to the Virgin, who wore a gown made from Mrs. Dutra's wedding dress and a wig of her nephew's curls.

Our Lady who came to evangelize the Indians was saved by her Indian converts!

Before Mrs. Dutra died, noted Sr. Celeste Pagliarulo, SND de N, in *Southern California Quarterly*, she asked that the statue be entrusted to Tulita Westfall, a Monterey artist and a descendant of José Manuel Boronda, a Spanish soldier in Alta California in Padre Serra's time. Mission Carmel was restored in the mid-1900s, and the statue came home. Once again, Our Lady wears her crown and holds her missing Infant — who had been found in the Royal Presidio Chapel snuggled in the arms of his foster father, a statue of Saint Joseph.

 ## Our Lady of Bethlehem

Devotion to Our Lady of Bethlehem became popular in Portugal during the fifteenth century, the Age of Discovery. Prince Henry the Navigator built a small chapel to the Virgin on the Tagus River near Lisbon, at the mouth of the Atlantic Ocean. Captains and sailors would spend the night here in prayer before their ship's departure the next day. Vasco da Gama paid his respects to Our Lady before and after his epic voyage and discovery of the Indies in 1497–99.

In thanksgiving for da Gama's discovery, King Manual I erected about 1501 the Jerónimos Monastery, a UNESCO World Heritage Site, where the old chapel once stood. Mariners continued to solicit Our Lady's protection in the magnificent monastery church. The piety spread to Spain and then to the New World.

The title Our Lady of Bethlehem honors the Blessed Mother at the Nativity of Jesus. Her feast is celebrated on December 25, Christmas Day. By her intercession many lands and their peoples were born again for the love of her Son, the Savior of the World.

Alaska

FAIRBANKS

52

Don't bet against Mary when you visit Fairbanks: She's known as a "holy roller" in these parts! Folks who bet against her in 1911 lost — that's part of the frontier lore at **Immaculate Conception Church**, located in historic downtown Fairbanks.

This charming story begins in 1904, when Fr. Francis Monroe, SJ, was sent to Fairbanks to establish a church for the booming town of gold prospectors, many of whom were Catholic. Since all the choice lots in the center of town were taken, the Jesuit missionary bought land on the south side of the Chena River and built a little frame church — the first Roman Catholic church in the Interior of Alaska. Two years later, St. Joseph's Hospital (now defunct) went up on the other side of the river.

Whenever the priests needed to minister to the hospital sick, or offer Mass for the Sisters of Providence of Montreal who staffed the hospital, they had to cross the Chena River twice — coming and going. It was not only a great inconvenience but also dangerous. During the bitter-cold winter months in Fairbanks, temperatures can plummet to sixty degrees below zero. So, the intrepid Father Monroe decided to move the thirty-by-sixty-five-foot structure across the river to be closer to the hospital.

One November day in 1911, after the Chena River had frozen over, Father Munroe and his teams of horses and men began rolling the little church on skids across the ice. According to church history, "Everyone in town turned out to watch!" Bets were placed; odds were the church wouldn't make it.

Just as the church was being lifted up the riverbank and onto its new basement foundation, a cable snapped. The crowds gasped. The winning bettors (or so they thought) had gold coins flashing in their eyes. But, wonder of wonders, Mary and a second cable held tight. The "little church that could" arrived safely at its new home, where it stands today. Three years later, the church roof was raised and a choir loft, belfry, and vestibule added. A two-story rectory was also built and attached to one side of the church.

Historic Immaculate Conception Church is lauded for its ornamental pressed tin and exquisite stained-glass windows (the finest in all Alaska, some say), including one window dedicated to early Catholic frontier women. A statue of Mary, attired in a blue robe with a hint of a smile on her face, stands over the entrance — a reminder to always "bet on Mary," whether you're moving a church or in need

Exterior — Immaculate Conception Church, Fairbanks, Alaska

of a miracle.

Come to Mary: 2 Doyon Place, Fairbanks, AK 99701. (907) 452-3533. iccfairbanks.org.

ACKNOWLEDGMENTS

This book began with a single word and a battalion of Mary's helpers who assisted with research. Librarians and archivists. Parish priests and secretaries. Monks and nuns. Shrine guardians and caretakers. Tourism bureaus. Authors of ages past who put pen to paper to preserve the histories and miraculous stories of these hallowed sites. Heaps of thanks cannot begin to express my deepest gratitude for your guidance and assistance. You are surely stars on Mary's mantle.

A special acknowledgment to the following people who offered help beyond measure:

Rosemary Alva and Fr. Brian Dinkel, IVE, Our Lady of Peace Church and Shrine, Santa Clara, California; Martha Abeyta, Our Lady of Guadalupe

Church, Conejos, Colorado; Sr. Roselle Santivasi, MSC, Mother Cabrini Shrine, Golden, Colorado; John Pearce, Ave Maria Shrine, Trinidad, Colorado; Sharon Heavens and Fr. Timothy M. Dolan, Shrine of Our Lady Queen of Peace, Holy Spirit Church, New Castle, Delaware; Maria Morera Johnson, National Shrine of Our Lady of Charity (Ermita de la Caridad), Miami, Florida; Mackenzie Tucker, National Shrine of Our Lady of La Leche, St. Augustine, Florida; Mary Jeanne Schumacher, Monte Cassino Shrine, Saint Meinrad Archabbey, St. Meinrad, Indiana; Fr. Brian Esarey and Sally J. Saalman Mosby, St. Augustine Church, Leopold, Indiana; Sr. Jan Craven, SP, Sisters of Providence, Saint Mary-of-the-Woods, Indiana; Terry Hegarty, Trinity Heights Queen of Peace Shrine, Sioux City, Iowa; Andy Milam, Shrine of the Grotto of the Redemption, West Bend, Iowa;

J. D. Benning (St. Benedict's Abbey) and Tom Hoopes, Benedictine College, Atchison, Kansas; Elmer Ronnebaum, St. Mary's Grotto, St. Mary's Church, St. Benedict, Kansas; Ruth May and Joleen Reeger, Our Lady of Lourdes Grotto, St. Mark the Evangelist Catholic Church, St. Marks, Kansas; Mitzi Ropollo and Meghan Sylvester, Madonna Chapel, Bayou Goula (Plaquemine), Louisiana; Mary Lee Harris, National Votive Shrine of Our Lady of Prompt Succor, New Orleans, Louisiana;

Keenan Aungst, National Shrine Grotto of Our Lady of Lourdes, Emmitsburg, Maryland; Fr. Joseph Tizio, CSsR, Basilica of Our Lady of Perpetual Help, Boston, Massachusetts; Cathy Brown-Kuba, Our Lady of the Woods Shrine, Mio, Michigan; Marvin Salzer and Kristi Warne, Assumption Chapel, Cold Spring, Minnesota; Patricia Grasher and Cindy Thele, Shrine of Our Lady Queen of Peace, St. John

Church, Leopold, Missouri; Angela Pancella, St. Francis Xavier College Church, St. Louis, Missouri; Marge Fenelon and Brenda Van Booven, Shrine of Our Lady of Sorrows, Starkenburg, Missouri; Colleen Meyer and Terri Todd, Historic St. Mary's Mission and St. Mary's Mission Church, Stevensville, Montana; Rhonda Kraft, Sondra L. Jonson, and Fr. Kenneth Wehrs, Our Lady of Fatima Shrine and St. Germanus Church, Arapahoe, Nebraska; Wanda Vint, Cathedral Basilica of St. Francis of Assisi, Santa Fe, New Mexico; Dave F. Ali, Basilica of Regina Pacis, Brooklyn, New York; Sr. Nancy Kaczmarek, GNSH, Our Lady of Victory National Shrine and Basilica, Lackawanna, New York; Sr. Debra Weina, SSJ-TOSF, Shrine of Our Lady of Czestochowa, Garfield Heights, Ohio; Fr. John Bamman, OFM Conv, Basilica and National Shrine of Our Lady of Consolation, Carey, Ohio; Bonnie Lee, Basilica and National Shrine of Our Lady of Lebanon, North Jackson, Ohio; Fr. Vidal Martínez, OSM, National Sanctuary of Our Sorrowful Mother (The Grotto), Portland, Oregon; Teresa Ogonowski and Fr. Timothy Tarnacki, OSPPE, National Shrine of Our Lady of Czestochowa, Doylestown, Pennsylvania; Mary Peterson, Miraculous Medal Shrine, Philadelphia, Pennsylvania; Fr. Jorge A. Gómez and Frances Silva, Basilica of Our Lady of San Juan del Valle National Shrine, San Juan, Texas; Sherry Berend and Barbara Hoff, St. Mary's Grotto, St. Mary's Catholic Church, Windthorst, Texas; Sr. Agnes Fischer, OSF, Sisters of St. Francis of the Holy Cross of Green Bay, National Shrine of Our Lady of Good Help, Champion, Wisconsin.

RESOURCES

NORTHEAST
Massachusetts
Basilica of Our Lady of Perpetual Help, Boston

- Basilica of Our Lady of Perpetual Help. https://www.bostonsbasilica.com.
- Byrne, CSsR, Rev. John F. *The Glories of Mary in Boston: A Memorial History of the Church of Our Lady of Perpetual Help (Mission Church) Roxbury, Mass. 1871-1921.* Boston, MA: Mission Church Press, 1921.

New York
Basilica of Regina Pacis, Brooklyn
- Basilica of Regina Pacis. https:// basilicaofreginapacis.org.

Historic Shrine of Maria Hilf, Cheektowaga
- Atwell, Glenn R. and Ronald Elmer Batt. *The Chapel: A Comprehensive History of the Chapel and Pilgrimage of Our Lady Help of Christians, Cheektowaga, New York and of the Alsatian Immigrant Community at Williamsville, New York.* Buffalo, NY: The Town of Cheektowaga and The Holling Press, Inc., 1979.
- Our Lady Help of Christians Roman Catholic Church. http://www.ourladyhelpofchristians .org/our-historic-chapel.html.

Our Lady of Victory National Shrine and Basilica, Lackawanna
- Anderson, Floyd. *Apostle of Charity: The Father Nelson Henry Baker Story.* Our Lady of Victory Homes of Charity, 1960.
- Gribble, CSC, Richard. *Father of the Fatherless: The Authorized Biography of Father Nelson Baker.* Mahwah, NJ: Paulist Press, 2011.
- OLV National Shrine and Basilica. https://www .olvbasilica.org/history-of-the-shrine.

MID-ATLANTIC
Delaware
Shrine of Our Lady Queen of Peace, New Castle
- https://www.holyspiritchurchde.org/our-lady -queen-of-peace-statue.

Maryland
National Shrine Grotto of Our Lady of Lourdes, Emmitsburg

- National Shrine Grotto of Our Lady of Lourdes. https://www.nsgrotto.org.
- *The Story of Our Lady's Grotto.* Emmitsburg, MD: Mount Saint Mary's University, n.d.

Pennsylvania
Assumption of the Blessed Virgin Mary Ukrainian Catholic Church, Centralia

- Assumption of the Blessed Virgin Mary Ukrainian Catholic Church. http://ukrarcheparchy.us/assumption-of-bvm-centralia.
- Hangley Jr., Bill. "A Town was Engulfed in Flames, but One Church Still Stands Today." *Reader's Digest.* December 2018/January 2019. https://www.rd.com/article/centralia-pennsylvania-assumption-ukrainian-church-saved-from-fire/.
- Quigley, Joan. *The Day the Earth Caved In: An American Mining Tragedy.* New York, NY: Random House, Inc., 2007.

National Shrine of Our Lady of Czestochowa, Doylestown

- Lorenc, OSPPE, Father Gabriel. *American Czestochowa.* Doylestown, PA: National Shrine of Our Lady of Czestochowa, 1989.
- National Shrine of Our Lady of Czestochowa, https://czestochowa.us.
- Reagan, President Ronald. Speech at National Shrine of Our Lady of Czestochowa, September 9, 1984: https://www.reaganlibrary.gov/archives/speech/remarks-polish

-festival-doylestown-pennsylvania.

Miraculous Medal Shrine, Philadelphia
- Dirvin, CM, Father Joseph. "Mary's Priest." *The Miraculous Medal, Father Skelly Memorial Edition*, September 1963.
- Miraculous Medal Shrine. https://miraculousmedal.org.
- "St. Catherine's Work." *The Miraculous Medal, Father Skelly Memorial Edition*, September 1963.

SOUTHEAST
Florida
Basilica of Saint Mary Star of the Sea, Key West
- Basilica of Saint Mary Star of the Sea. https://stmarykeywest.com.
- Bernreuter, Bob J. *Star of the Sea: A History of the Basilica St. Mary Star of the Sea*. Key West, FL: Key West Publishing, 2012.
- Knight, Marcy. "Deliver us from storms: How a grotto, prayers seem to keep Key West safe from destructive hurricanes." *Florida Catholic*, August 19, 2013. https://www.miamiarch .org/CatholicDiocese.php?op =Article_13814162647850.

National Shrine of Our Lady of Charity (Ermita de la Caridad), Miami
- Alvarez, Lizette. "400 Years Later, Still Revered in Cuba (and Miami)." *New York Times*, September 9, 2012. https://www.nytimes.com/2012 /09/10/us/la-virgen-de-la-caridad -anniversary-celebrated-in-miami.html.
- Archdiocese of Miami. "Our Lady of Charity National Shrine." https://www.miamiarch.org

/CatholicDiocese.php?op=
Church_531417225934_main.

- Hemingway, Ernest. *The Old Man and the Sea.*
  New York, NY: Scribner, 1952.
- Morera Johnson, Maria. *Our Lady of Charity:
  How a Cuban Devotion to Mary Helped Me Grow
  in Faith and Love.* Notre Dame, IN: Ave Maria
  Press, 2019.
- National Shrine of Our Lady of Charity (Ermita
  de la Caridad). https://ermita.org.

National Shrine of Our Lady of La Leche, St. Augustine

- Amberg, Marion. "Baby Wanted: The Shrine of
  Our Lady of La Leche." *St. Anthony Messenger,*
  May 2006.
- Geiger, Matthew J. *Mission of Nombre de Dios,
  Shrine of Our Lady of La Leche, St. Augustine
  Florida, A Brief History.* Mission of Nombre de
  Dios, 2003.
- National Shrine of Our Lady of La Leche.
  https://missionandshrine.org.

Georgia
Catholic Shrine of the Immaculate Conception, Atlanta

- Catholic Shrine of the Immaculate Conception.
  https://www.catholicshrineatlanta.org.
- Colley, Van Buren. *History of the Diocesan Shrine
  of the Immaculate Conception.* Atlanta, GA: The
  Diocesan Shrine of the Immaculate Conception, 1955.

Louisiana
Madonna Chapel, Bayou Goula (Plaquemine)

- Amberg, Marion. "Little Chapels, Big Stories of
  Faith." *St. Anthony Messenger,* February 2007.

- Fama, Anthony P. *Plaquemine: A Glimpse of the Early Years.* n.p., 2004.
- Grace, Albert L. *The Heart of the Sugar Bowl: The Story of Iberville.* Baton Rouge, LA: The Franklin Press, 1946.
- Iberville Parish Tourism. https://map .ibervilleparish.com/listing/madonna-chapel.

National Votive Shrine of Our Lady of Prompt Succor, New Orleans

- Annals of the Ursuline Convent, New Orleans, Louisiana. https://www.shrineofourladyofpromptsuccor .com/mass-of-thanksgiving-; https://storage .googleapis.com/production -constantcontact-v1-0-2/072/341072 /dqbJXDvN/f93ad026e37b4345b8ff080c2d7bc459
- Kilmeade, Brian, and Don Yaeger. *Andrew Jackson and the Miracle of New Orleans: The Battle that Shaped America's Destiny.* New York, NY: Penguin Random House, 2017.
- Muller, CSC, Brother Gerald. *Our Lady Comes to New Orleans.* Austin, TX: Brothers of Holy Cross Southwest Province, n.d.
- National Votive Shrine of Our Lady of Prompt Succor, https://www .shrineofourladyofpromptsuccor.com.

Virgin Island, Pierre Part

- St. Joseph the Worker Church. https://sjworker .org.
- Templet, Wildly L. *Pierre Part – Belle Riviere Down Home.* Pierre Part, LA: self-published, 1999.

North Carolina
Abbey Basilica of Mary Help of Christians, Belmont

- Abbey Basilica of Mary Help of Christians. https://belmontabbey.org/about-us/#the-basilica.
- Baumstein, OSB, Dom Paschal. *My Lord of Belmont: A Biography of Leo Haid*. Belmont, NC: The Archives of Belmont Abbey, 1985.

MIDWEST
Illinois
Holy Family Church, Chicago

- Holy Family Church. https://www.holyfamilychicago.org.
- Little, Darnell. "Dead Cows Tell No Tales." *Chicago Tribune*, November 9, 1996. https://www.chicagotribune.com/news/ct-xpm-1996-11-09-9701150573-story.html.
- Mills, Steve. "Mrs. O'Leary, Cow Cleared by City Council Committee." *Chicago Tribune*, October 6, 1997. https://www.chicagotribune.com/news/ct-xpm-1997-10-06-9710070022-story.html.
- Mulkerins, SJ, Brother Thomas M. *Holy Family Parish Chicago: Priests and People*. Chicago, IL: Universal Press, 1923; https://archive.org/details/holyfamilyparish00mulk.
- Skerrett, Ellen. *Born in Chicago: A History of Chicago's Jesuit University*. Chicago, IL: Loyola Press, 2008.

Indiana
St. Augustine Church, Leopold

- Archdiocese of Indianapolis. https://www.archindy.org/parishes/listings/089.html.
- Cornwell, Patricia Happel. "Perry County parish

celebrates 175 years of faith." *The Criterion*, September 21, 2012. https://www.archindy.org/criterion/local/2012/09-21/perry.html.

Shrine of Christ's Passion, St. John
- Jardine, Gail. *Our Lady of the New Millennium: One Man's Dream*. St. Charles, IL: JMJ Home Corporation, n.d.
- Marlan, Tori. "Carl Demma's Mighty Metal Madonna." *Chicago Reader*, February 15, 2001. https://www.chicagoreader.com/chicago/carl-demmas-mighty-metal-madonna/Content?oid=904608.
- Shrine of Christ's Passion. https://shrineofchristspassion.org.

Sisters of Providence, Saint Mary-of-the-Woods
- Sisters of Providence of Saint Mary-of-the-Woods. https://spsmw.org.
- Pohlman, OP, Sister Ann Paula. "Mother's devotion to Our Lady of Providence lives on," June 3, 2016. https://spsmw.org/author/appohlman.

Monte Cassino Shrine, St. Meinrad
- Kleber, OSB, STD, Albert. *History of St. Meinrad Archabbey 1854–1954*. St. Meinrad, IN: St. Meinrad Archabbey, 1954.
- *Monte Cassino Shrine 1870–1995*, an anniversary booklet published by Saint Meinrad Archabbey.
- Saint Meinrad Archabbey. https://www.saintmeinrad.org/the-monastery/monte-cassino-shrine.

Iowa
Trinity Heights Queen of Peace Shrine, Sioux City

- Cooper, Bernard (Beanie). *The Miracle of Trinity Heights*. Queen of Peace, Inc., 2011.
- Trinity Heights Queen of Peace Shrine. http://www.trinityheights.com.

Shrine of the Grotto of the Redemption, West Bend
- Amberg, Marion. Recorded onsite interview with Father Louis H. Greving, September 29, 2001.
- Greving, Father Louis H. *A Pictorial Story of the Grotto of the Redemption*. Grotto of the Redemption, 1993.
- Hutchinson, Duane. *Grotto Father: Artist-Priest of the West Bend Grotto*. Lincoln, NE: Foundation Books, 1989.
- Shrine of the Grotto of the Redemption. https://www.westbendgrotto.com.

Kansas
Benedictine College, Atchison
- Benedictine College. https://www.benedictine.edu; https://www.benedictine.edu/faith-life/memorare/miracles.
- Lemke, Father Henry. *A Warrior in God's Service: The Memoirs of Peter Henry Lemke 1796–1882*. Atchison, KS: St. Benedict's Abbey, 2007.
- Naumann, Archbishop Joseph. "Use the 'Memorare' to approach Jesus through Mary." *The Leaven*, January 8, 2010. http://theleaven.org/column-use-the-memorare-to-approach-jesus-through-mary/.

Our Lady of Lourdes Grotto, St. Marks
- Eck, Brenda M. "Every year is Marian Year at St. Mark's." *The Catholic Advance*, May 5, 1988.

- St. Mark the Evangelist Catholic Church. https://stmarkks.org.

St. Mary's Grotto, St. Benedict, Kansas
- Anderson, Marc and Julie. "Weekly rosary at St. Mary's grotto honors long tradition." *The Leaven*, June 4, 2021. http://theleaven.org /weekly-rosary-at-st-marys-grotto-honors -long-tradition/.
- St. Mary's Church. https://stmarystbenedict .org/.
- *St. Mary's Catholic Parish, St. Benedict, Kansas 1859–2009: Faith Moves Us Forward*, St. Benedict, KS: St. Mary's Parish, 2009.

Michigan
Our Lady of the Woods Shrine, Mio
- *Rejoicing in Faith*, Our Lady of the Woods Shrine, Fall 2019. https://bdf613d7-c906-47e5-98de -a2dbec7e30c3.filesusr.com/ugd/ad7c27 _59feb5110a324e18a4dea094b12182ac.pdf.
- *Our Lady of the Woods Shrine*, a souvenir booklet. n.p., 1959.
- Our Lady of the Woods Shrine and Saint Mary Catholic Church, https://www.olwshrine.org.

Minnesota
Assumption Chapel, Cold Spring
- Saint Boniface Parish. *Amid Hills of Granite, A Spring of Faith: A History of Saint Boniface Parish, Cold Spring, Minnesota, 1878–1978.* Centennial Committee, 1978.
- Smithsonian National Museum of Natural History. https://www.eol.org/pages/500065 /articles; https://naturalhistory.si.edu

/education/teaching-resources/paleontology /extinction-over-time.

- *St. Paul Dispatch.* Various news reports in its April 9, April 27, April 28, May 2, and May 3, 1877 editions.
- Voigt, Robert J. *The Story of Mary and the Grasshoppers.* n.p., 1991.
- Wallfahrtskirche Maria Hilf. https://www .mariahilfberg-amberg.de.
- Wilder, Laura Ingalls. *On the Banks of Plum Creek.* 1937. Rev. ed. New York, NY: HarperCollins, 1953.

Cathedral of the Holy Spirit, New Ulm

- Cathedral of the Holy Spirit. http://www .holycrossafc.org/cathedral-of-the-holy-trinity -history.html.
- Radzilowski, John. *Bells Across the Prairie: 125 Years of Holy Trinity Catholic Church, New Ulm, Minnesota.* Cathedral of the Holy Trinity, 1995.

Missouri
Shrine of Our Lady Queen of Peace, Leopold

- Proctor, OSC, Sister Patricia. *101 Inspirational Stories of the Rosary.* Spokane, WA: Franciscan Monastery of Saint Clare, 2003.
- St. John Church. https://stjohnchurchleopold .com.

Our Lady of the Rivers Shrine, Portage Des Sioux

- Palmer, Faith. "The Blessing of the Fleet." *Missouri Life,* May–August 1984.
- Our Lady of the Rivers Shrine, https:// ourladyoftheriversshrine.org.

Shrine of Our Lady of Sorrows, Starkenburg
- Excerpt from the hymn "To Jesus Christ Our Sovereign King" — Copyright Irene Mueller, used by permission.
- Shrine of Our Lady of Sorrows. http://historicshrine.com.

St. Francis Xavier College Church, St. Louis
- Laveille, S.J., E. *The Life of Father De Smet, S.J.* Chicago, IL: Loyola University Press, 1981.
- St. Francis Xavier Church. https://sfxstl.org.

Nebraska
Our Lady of Fatima Shrine, Arapahoe
- Arapahoe Chamber of Commerce. http://www .arapahoe-ne.com/attractions/shrine.htm.
- *Southern Nebraska Register.* "Fatima centennial to be celebrated at Arapahoe parish, shrine." May 5, 2017. https://www.lincolndiocese.org /news/diocesan-news/8992-fatima-centennial -to-be-celebrated-at-arapahoe-parish-shrine.

Ohio
Basilica and National Shrine of Our Lady of Consolation, Carey
- Basilica and National Shrine of Our Lady of Consolation. https://www.olcshrine.com.
- Facebook: https://www.facebook.com /olcshrinecarey/?ref=pages_you_manage.
- Hines, OFM Conv, Brother Jeffrey. *A History of the Basilica and National Shrine of Our Lady of Consolation 1868 to 2012.* Conventual Franciscans of Our Lady of Consolation.

Shrine of Our Lady of Czestochowa, Garfield Heights

- "History of the Icon of Our Lady of Czestochowa in Garfield Heights, Ohio," a pamphlet in the Archives of the Sisters of St. Joseph of the Third Order of St. Francis, Stevens Point, Wisconsin.

Basilica and National Shrine of Our Lady of Lebanon, North Jackson

- Basilica and National Shrine of Our Lady of Lebanon. https://www.ourladyoflebanonshrine.com.
- Celebration booklet *Golden Jubilee National Shrine of Our Lady of Lebanon and Consecration and Dedication of the Basilica of Christ, the Prince of Peace*, 2014.

Wisconsin
National Shrine of Our Lady of Good Help, Champion

- Excerpt from "The Chapel: Our Lady of Good Help" by Sister Dominica Shallow, OSF. © The Sisters of St. Francis of the Holy Cross, Green Bay, WI.
- National Shrine of Our Lady of Good Help, https://championshrine.org.
- Pernin, Reverend Peter. *The Great Peshtigo Fire: An Eyewitness Account*. Madison, WI: State Historical Society of Wisconsin, 1999.

MOUNTAIN WEST
Colorado
Our Lady of Guadalupe Church, Conejos

- Our Lady of Guadalupe Parish. http://www.ologp.com.
- Smith, Daniel. "Places: Our Lady of Guadalupe

Church." *Colorado Central Magazine*, December 1, 2017. https://coloradocentralmagazine.com /places-our-lady-of-guadalupe-church/.

Mother Cabrini Shrine, Golden
- Miceli, MSC, Mother Ignatius. *Cabrinian Colorado Missions*. Boulder, Colorado: D & K Printing, 1996.
- Mother Cabrini Shrine. https://mothercabrinishrine.org.

Ave Maria Shrine, Trinidad
- Most Holy Trinity Roman Catholic Church. https://www.trinidadcatholic.org.

Montana
Our Lady of the Rockies, Butte
- Lee, LeRoy. *Our Lady Builds a Statue*. N.p., 1992.
- *Montana Standard*. "Our Lady of the Rockies timeline." December 20, 2015, updated January 8, 2018. https://mtstandard.com /news/local/our-lady-of-the-rockies -timeline/article_a7bd8c9e-9541 -56b3-998c-ff59896930aa.html.
- *Montana Standard*. "Our Lady of the Rockies 'Did You Know?'" December 20, 2015. https:// mtstandard.com/news/local/our-lady-of-the -rockies-did-you-know/article_c9365f58-7fb1 -5e7f-8146-37553be23bae.html.
- Our Lady of the Rockies. https://www .ourladyoftherockies.net.

Historic St. Mary's Mission, Stevensville
- De Smet, Pierre-Jean. *Origin, Progress, and Prospects of the Catholic Mission to the Rocky Moun-*

tains. Philadelphia PA: M. Fithian, 1843.

- Evans, Lucylle H. *St. Mary's in the Rocky Mountains: A History of the Cradle of Montana's Culture.* Stevensville, MT: Montana Creative Consultants, 1975.
- Historic St. Mary's Mission. https://www.saintmarysmission.org.

SOUTHWEST
New Mexico
Cathedral Basilica of St. Francis of Assisi, Santa Fe

- 1712 Fiesta Proclamation. State Records Center and Archives, Spanish Archives of New Mexico, Series I, no. 179. http://2013archive.santafefiesta.org/wp-content/uploads/2012/07/Santa-Fe-Feista-1712-Proclimation.pdf.
- Amberg, Marion. *Shrines and Wonders: The Pilgrim's Guide to Santa Fe and Northern New Mexico.* Phoenix, AZ: Amor Deus Publishing, 2016.
- Cathedral Basilica of St. Francis of Assisi. https://www.cbsfa.org.
- Chavez, Fray Angelico. *La Conquistadora: The Autobiography of an Ancient Statue.* Santa Fe, NM: Sunstone Press, 1975, Revised Edition, 1983.
- Melzer, Richard. "Kidnapping La Conquistadora, 1973." *La Crónica de Nuevo México*, December 2004. https://digitalrepository.unm.edu/cgi/viewcontent.cgi?article=1063&context=lacronica.
- Santa Fe Fiesta. https://www.santafefiesta.org.
- *The Santa Fe Cathedral of St. Francis of Assisi.* Original edition 1947, revised 1968, 1978, 1987,

and 1995. n.p.

Santuario de Guadalupe, Santa Fe

- Amberg, Marion. *Shrines and Wonders: The Pilgrim's Guide to Santa Fe and Northern New Mexico*. Phoenix, AZ: Amor Deus Publishing, 2016.
- Santuario de Guadalupe. https://santuariodeguadalupesantafe.com.
- "Restoration at Guadalupe." *The Santa Fean Magazine,* July 1977.

Texas

Basilica of Our Lady of San Juan del Valle National Shrine, San Juan

- Azpiazu, OMI, Father Joseph. "Virgen de San Juan del Valle Shrine." *Handbook of Texas Online,* published by the Texas State Historical Association. https://www.tshaonline.org/handbook/entries/virgen-de-san-juan-del-valle-shrine.
- Basilica of Our Lady of San Juan del Valle National Shrine. https://www.olsjbasilica.org/about-us/history.
- Cruz, Joan Carroll. *Miraculous Images of Our Lady: 100 Famous Catholic Portraits and Statues.* Charlotte, NC: TAN Books, 1993.
- *Virgen de San Juan Shrine, San Juan, Texas.* Hackensack, NJ: 1980.

St. Mary's Grotto, Windthorst, Texas

- Kocks-Burgess, Jenara. "The story of a grotto, a small town, and the intercession of Our Lady." *North Texas Catholic,* June 29, 2017.
- Lindemann, William ("Rusty"). "History of the

Small Grotto Built by Charles Lindeman."
- Pruitt, Bernadette. "Veterans forever grateful." *The Dallas Morning News*, November 9, 2001.
- St. Mary's Catholic Church, https://stmarysstboniface.com.

PACIFIC WEST
Alaska
Immaculate Conception Church, Fairbanks
- https://iccfairbanks.org/church-history.

California
Carmel Mission Basilica, Carmel
- Carmel Mission Basilica, https://carmelmission.org.
- Morgado, Martin J. *Junípero Serra's Legacy*. Pacific Grove, CA: Mount Carmel, 1987.
- Orfalea, Gregory. *Journey to the Sun: Junípero Serra's Dream and the Founding of California*. New York, NY: Scribner, 2014.
- Pagliarulo, SDN de N, Sister Celeste. "Harry Downie and the Contents of Mission San Carlos Borromeo, 1931–1967." *Southern California Quarterly*, Spring 2005, Vol. 87, No. 1.

Our Lady of Peace Church and Shrine, Santa Clara
- Alva, Rosemary. *Our Lady's Way: The Story of Our Lady of Peace Church and Shrine*. Santa Clara, CA: Our Lady of Peace Church & Shrine, 2019.
- Our Lady of Peace Church and Shrine. https://www.olop-shrine.org.

Oregon
National Sanctuary of Our Sorrowful Mother (The Grotto), Portland

- Order of Servites of Mary. https://thegrotto.org/the-servites/.
- *The Grotto: A place of peace, prayer, and natural beauty, A Self-Guided Tour.* n.d., published by The Grotto.
- *The Grotto.* A pictorial book, n.d., published by The Grotto.
- The National Sanctuary of Our Sorrowful Mother. https://thegrotto.org.

INDEX OF FEATURED MARIAN SITES AND DEVOTIONS

Our Lady of the Rockies
Butte, Montana, site 40.
Our Lady of the Rosary
Santa Clara, California, site 50; New Castle, Delaware, site 9; Atlanta, Georgia, site 11; Sioux City, Iowa, site 31; St. Benedict, Kansas, site 38; St. Marks, Kansas, site 39; New Ulm, Minnesota, site 29; Leopold, Missouri, site 35; Portage Des Sioux, Missouri, site 33; Arapahoe, Nebraska, site 36.
Our Lady of San Juan of the Lakes
San Juan, Texas, site 46.
Our Lady of Sorrows
Starkenburg, Missouri, site 32; Portland, Oregon, site 49.
Our Lady Queen of Peace
New Castle, Delaware, site 9; Sioux City, Iowa, site 31; Leopold, Missouri, site 35.
Our Lady of Victory
Lackawanna, New York, site 1.
Regina Pacis
Brooklyn, New York, site 3.

PHOTO CREDITS

NORTHEAST
New York
1. Courtesy of OLV National Shrine & Basilica, Lackawanna, New York
2. Courtesy of Historic Shrine of Maria Hilf, Cheektowaga, New York
3. Courtesy of the Basilica of Regina Pacis, Brooklyn, New York

Massachusetts
4. Courtesy of the Basilica of Our Lady of Perpetual Help, Boston, Massachusetts

MID-ATLANTIC
Pennsylvania
5. Courtesy of the Central Association of the Miraculous Medal
6. Courtesy of Fr. Timothy Tarnacki, National Shrine of Our Lady of Czestochowa, Doylestown, Pennsylvania
7. Adobe Stock

Maryland
8. Courtesy of the National Shrine Grotto of Our Lady of Lourdes, Emmitsburg, Maryland

Delaware
9. Courtesy of Holy Spirit Church, New Castle, Delaware

SOUTHEAST
North Carolina
10. Courtesy of Belmont Abbey College

Georgia
11. Public domain via WikiArt.

Florida
12. Courtesy of Mission Nombre de Dios, Saint Augustine, Florida
13. Adobe Stock
14. Courtesy of the Basilica of Saint Mary Star of the Sea, Key West,

Florida

Louisiana
15. Courtesy of National Votive Shrine of Our Lady of Prompt Succor, New Orleans, Louisiana
16. Courtesy of Duane Breaux
17. Courtesy of Iberville Parish

MIDWEST
Michigan
18. Courtesy of Our Lady of the Woods Shrine, Mio, Michigan

Ohio
19. Courtesy of Allison Barrick
20. Used with permission of the Conventual Franciscan Friars
21. Used with permission from the Archives of the Sisters of St. Joseph of the Third Order of St. Francis, Stevens Point, Wisconsin

Indiana
22. Courtesy of Sisters of Providence, Saint Mary-of-the-Woods, Indiana
23. Courtes of Shrine of Christ's Passion, St. John, Indiana
24. Courtesy of Saint Meinrad Archabbey, St. Meinrad, Indiana
25. Courtesy of St. Augustine Church, Leopold, Indiana

Wisconsin
26. Courtesy of the National Shrine of Our Lady of Good Help, Champion, Wisconsin

Illinois
27. Courtesy of Church of the Holy Family, Chicago, Illinois

Minnesota
28. Glenn M. Harden, CC BY-SA 3.0, via Wikimedia Commons
29. Courtesy of Holy Cross Area Faith Community

Iowa
30. Adobe Stock
31. Courtesy of Trinity Heights Queen of Peace Shrine, Sioux City, Iowa

Missouri
32. Courtesy of the Shrine of Our Lady of Sorrows, Starkenburg, Missouri
33. Public domain via Wikimedia Commons
34. Courtesy of the Saint Louis University Archives
35. Courtesy of the Shrine of Our Lady Queen of Peace, Leopold, Missouri

Nebraska
36. Photograph by Sherry Cacy. Courtesy of St. Germanus Church/Our Lady of Fatima Shrine

Kansas
37. Courtesy of Benedictine College
38. Courtesy of Elmer Ronnebaum
39. Courtesy of Dale Stelz

MOUNTAIN WEST
Montana
40. Adobe Stock
41. Forest Service Northern Region from Missoula, Montana, USA, Public domain, via Wikimedia Commons

Colorado
42. Adobe Stock
43. Adobe Stock
44. Courtesy of Our Lady of Guadalupe Parish, Conejos, Colorado

SOUTHWEST
Texas
45. Courtesy of St. Mary's Church, Windthorst, Texas
46. Adobe Stock

New Mexico
47. Courtesy of Marion Amberg
48. Courtesy of Marion Amberg

PACIFIC WEST
Oregon
49. Courtesy of The Grotto, Portland, Oregon

California
50. Courtesy of Our Lady of Peace Church and Shrine, Santa Clara, California
51. Adobe Stock

Alaska
52. Adobe Stock

ABOUT THE AUTHOR

Marion Amberg is an award-winning journalist and book author specializing in human interest and religion topics. She is known for her "sense of the odd and curious" and for her humorous and engaging writing style. She is the author of the best-selling *Monuments, Marvels, and Miracles: A Traveler's Guide to Catholic America*, the first book in the Catholic America travel series, also from OSV.

While researching this book, the author discovered a Marian miracle in her family lineage at Amberg, Germany. In 1634, Maria Hilf (Mary's Help) delivered the Bavarian town from the bubonic plague, a scourge that had wiped out whole sections of Amberg. Without Maria Hilf's miraculous intervention at Amberg, she and her family might not be here today.

Ave Maria!

You might also like:

Monuments, Marvels, and Miracles: A Traveler's Guide to Catholic America

By Marion Amberg

America's got faith! You'll find it in every state — in grand cathedrals and tiny chapels, in miracle shrines and underwater statues, and even in blessed dirt. Finding these sacred places hasn't been easy, until now!

The companion to *Mary's Miracles*, this book takes you to more than 500 of the country's most intriguing holy sites, each with a riveting story to tell.

Organized by state and region, *Monuments, Marvels, and Miracles* can help you easily plan your vacation or pilgrimage, and find sites close to you that you've never heard of. Chapters also include Catholic trivia and color photos. Websites, phone numbers, addresses, and other pertinent information are included.

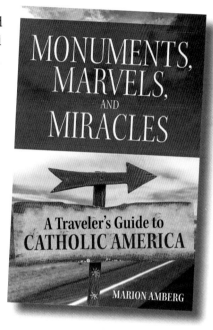

Available at
OSVCatholicBookstore.com
or wherever books are sold